I0803774

TOLEDO'S HISTORIC FARMERS' MARKET

TOLEDO'S HISTORIC FARMERS' MARKET

TRINI L. WENNINGER

THE History PRESS

Published by The History Press
Charleston, SC 29403
www.historypress.net

Front cover: Painting by Melinda Hallenbeck, inspired by a vintage photo of the Toledo Farmers' Market because the woman's "posture and gesture of kindness radiates pride and nostalgia." Raised in Toledo, Melinda attended Lourdes College and majored in psychology and art. She is currently attending Mount Mary College in Milwaukee, Wisconsin, and training for a master's in art therapy and counseling.

First published 2011

Manufactured in the United States

ISBN 978.1.60949.375.2

Library of Congress Cataloging-in-Publication Data

Wenninger, Trini L.
Toledo's historic farmers' market / Trini L. Wenninger.
p. cm.
Includes bibliographical references.
ISBN 978-1-60949-375-2
1. Toledo Farmers' Market. 2. Farmers' markets--Ohio--Toledo. 3. Farm produce--Ohio--Toledo--Marketing. 4. Cooking--Ohio--Toledo. I. Title.
HF5472.U7T65 2011
381'.410977113--dc23
2011033916

Contents

Acknowledgements	7
Introduction	9
Farmers' Markets	13
The Way of the Farmer	17
Toledo Farmers' Market History	27
Vendors	53
Recipes	79
What Is in Season in Ohio?	147
What Is a CSA?	151
Visiting the Toledo Farmers' Market	153
Epilogue	157
Notes	163
Selected Bibliography	171
About the Author	175

Acknowledgements

I am grateful to those who are the Toledo Farmers' Market.[1] I appreciate their willingness to open their hearts and share their stories with me. Many invited me to their farms, their gardens, their greenhouses and even into their homes. I have learned plenty and gained several friendships from the last few months, and for this I am thankful.

I wish to thank my editor, Joseph Gartrell, for suggesting a farmers' market book. Without his foresight, this book would not have taken shape. And to my mom, Debbie, who kept bugging me to write another book. Okay, Mom, here it is.

A book on the Toledo Farmers' Market could only be written with the help of many. I am grateful for Eleanor Billau, who clipped and saved articles and took photographs at the market through the years. She graciously shared those articles and photographs with me and sent me home with a bag full of history. Her collection became invaluable to this project, and for that I am truly indebted.

Many thanks go to my husband, Ken Wenninger, and to my friend Jodi Ashoftehfard for reading drafts of the manuscript and providing me with valuable feedback; and to my many Facebook friends, who helped vote on recipes and suggested information to include. I also appreciate the time senior editor Jaime Muehl spent whipping my manuscript into shape.

I really thought there was no one who loved horses more than my mom until I met Rose Main. I would not be surprised if one day we find out they are long-lost cousins. I am thankful to know Rose. She has been enthusiastic about the book and has given me encouragement from the start. She gave me the push I needed to get through some of the rougher days.

Acknowledgements

A big thanks to Katie Thomas, for not only sharing what she remembered about the market but also sharing memories of growing up in the South and her move to Toledo after World War II. She is an amazing woman.

I appreciate Dan Madigan and Becky Keil Kornmeier for allowing me access to what old documents they had locked away in the office and for answering my many questions. I am honored to know Elizabeth Bergman, whose dedication is inspiring. I was thankful to always see Amy Hendricks on Saturdays (she met me with a smile and inquired about the book's progress) and Debbie Wines, with whom I think, if time allowed, I could share chicken stories all day long.

A special thanks to Roger Zielinski for giving me advice on herbs and the heirloom tomatoes that have brought character to my garden. I appreciate the talks Lori Diver, Brian Jentzen and I had about food production and the direction the market is taking and J.P. Rady, for his constant encouragement and appreciation for history.

I cannot forget Ralph and Gini Behrendt, Betty and Max Jeffers, Judy Peper, Rachel Stanton, George Dabrunz, Scott Dabrunz, Tim Dabrunz, the Billau family, Leslie Jackson, the Wenz family, Josh Main, Fred Main, Hazel Schaller, Gary and Carolyn Ackerman, Brandon Parran, Shannon Marruquin, Diana and David DeBacker, Jacquie Olender, Andy Keil, Dennis Dickey, Leslie Miller, Shannon Marruquin, Ralph and Sheila Schlatter, Kelly Hewitt, Tylor Noel, Julie Jordan, Amelia Contreras, Elizabeth Fallon, Evelyn Keil, Ed and Lynne Weiland, Tom and Margie Lumbrezer, Carolyn Witt, Karen and Max Freytag, the Carpenter family, Louise Mikesell-Wireman, Konstantinos Konstandas, Pam Poeth, Linda Barrows, Matt Osborn, Emily Prasuhn, Tammy Saunders, Ilene Fruth, Congresswoman Marcy Kaptur, Wilma Ott and Jan Campbell.

A special thanks to Annette Fink and Melinda Hallenbeck for submitting art for this book. The wonderful painting Melinda created for the cover is extraordinary and better than I could have imagined.

I would like to thank my husband, Ken, and my daughter, Leia, for allowing me time to explore and time to write. They had more daddy-daughter dates than imaginable over the last few months.

It is nearly impossible to personally thank everyone who has helped with the completion of this book. To those I did not specifically name, I give you thanks for your help and for being part of Toledo Farmers' Market history.

Introduction

Many from my generation were raised on convenience foods. Our parents, for the most part, gave up baking and cooking for the sake of convenience. Food manufacturers took advantage of this and offered time-saving food preparation in their advertising. The food industry took over the family dinner.

Many of our parents themselves were raised on TV dinners and boxed, canned and frozen foods—staples in their childhood homes. Decade by decade, the food industry changed the standard American diet from unadulterated food consumed close to the source to heavily processed food items. It was estimated that in 2010, 50 percent of all meals were eaten away from home, with one in five breakfasts being from McDonald's.[2] Fewer and fewer people are fixing nutritious meals at home, and cooking is quickly becoming a lost art.

Even though genetics plays a role in health, eating the new standard American diet full of chemicals, fillers and preservatives took its toll on me. After conventional medical treatment failed to help with health concerns, I became obsessed with the quality of food I was consuming. Making most of my food at home was the only way I knew what I was eating and could ensure that I was avoiding as many chemicals, fillers and preservatives as possible. I became a label reader and started frequenting farmers' markets. I started buying most of my vegetables and meats from local farmers and started taking my daughter to pick-your-own fields and orchards. I started gardening, and now we raise chickens in our backyard so we have our own fresh eggs. I learned to can and freeze fruits and vegetables and slowly regained a sense of connection with my food. I made food a priority in my life, dedicating more of my time and energy to healthy food.

I discovered how wonderful farmers' markets are and am thrilled to have several large markets so close to home. At the farmers' markets, I can buy potatoes and hand my money to the woman who dug them from the dirt, and I can buy apples from the man who picked them from his orchard. I can buy honey from the woman who extracted the gooey sweetener from the hive and beef from the man who raised the cow. I can be assured that I am getting produce picked at its peak of freshness and not gassed, dipped, sprayed, radiated and waxed. I can find artisan cheeses, breads and fresh-baked goods, soaps and the perfect gift at the farmers' market. There are vendors who have taken their passions and their hobbies and created businesses of their own, and they are more than willing to share what they know about what they sell.

Through this journey, I have met several families who, like mine, are striving to reconnect with our past and wish to bring wholesome meals to our tables. We want to give our children the pleasure of tasting a flavorful tomato or a super sweet strawberry. We want to support the stewards of this land. The farmers' market has been the beginning for many of us. It has been a place to learn, to reach out and to educate.

As I learned more about the farmers at the Toledo Farmers' Market and their history, I continued to seek more information concerning the changes in agriculture. I wanted to know how it affected the farmers I met and food production through the years. The more I researched, the more complex it seemed. The history of agriculture and food production is not simple. There are many factors that affect agriculture and food production—technological advancements, societal expectations, marketing and government regulations, to name a few. Even with the complexity involved, I have made several connections. So much so that when I visited an Amish dairy farm in May 2011, I was not surprised to learn they were providing milk for Dean Foods.[3]

In this book you will find the history of Toledo's Farmers' Market combined with photos, recipes, cooking and baking hints, shopping tips and other useful information. I am sure you will enjoy a look back at the history of Toledo's Farmers' Market and have a fun time trying the recipes and utilizing the baking tips and cooking hints. The recipes in this book were inspired by the market, and much of the book's history relies heavily on newspaper clippings and the stories shared by the vendors. At times, this proved difficult; newspaper clippings can be sparse, and human memory is not always the best source.

The Ackerman family enjoying winter on the farm. *Courtesy of the Ackerman family.*

This book is certainly not a complete history of the market, but it provides a sampling of many more stories out there to be discovered. I hope this book will spark a renewed interest and encourage those who remember the Toledo Farmers' Market to step forward with their memories. My writing schedule did not coordinate perfectly with that of the growing seasons and the ebb and flow of the market. The lives of the farmers revolve around planting and harvesting and are affected by all the weather in between. Their time and my time was limited, and I was unable to hunt down everyone involved with the market or all those who played roles in its history and development. This exemplifies well how the market is constantly changing, continually being affected by the lives of those involved, the weather and the seasons. I cannot expect a June strawberry in November, so with this in mind, I believe a second volume is warranted.

Farmers' Markets

Kind hearts are the gardens,
Kind thoughts are the roots,
Kind words are the blossoms,
Kind deeds are the fruits.
—Henry Wadsworth Longfellow

Farmers' markets began as a way for farmers to sell their produce directly to the customers. Through the years, as food production became increasingly industrialized, the markets were replaced with supermarkets. Advancements in technology—such as transportation, storage facilities and mass merchandising—changed the way Americans ate and the way they shopped. People were no longer making their own jellies and preserves and no longer buying large quantities of fruits and vegetables to can and freeze.

However, in the past few years, there has been a growing interest in once again obtaining fresh products straight from the farm, and farmers' markets are regaining strength. These markets continue to provide access to locally grown, fresh produce and other farm products. As food writer Mary Alice Powell attests, "Once an appetite for locally grown seasonal produce is developed, it is nearly impossible to eat—let alone enjoy—tomatoes, watermelon, and sweet corn in winter when we know they have had a long trip from distant fields."[4]

In August 2010, the U.S. Department of Agriculture listed 6,132 farmers' markets across the country. This was a 16 percent increase from 2009. Each year, markets across the country have increased in numbers since the National Farmers Market Directory has been collecting self-reported information starting in 1994.

By December 2010, the National Farmers Market Directory of the U.S. Department of Agriculture listed 898 winter markets operating between November and March. Ohio boasted thirty-four winter markets that offered consumers access to locally grown food and other market goods. The Toledo Farmers' Market was one of these markets, with several regular vendors operating through the cold winter months, drawing approximately three hundred visitors on Saturdays.

Farmers' markets vary throughout the country. Some are set up on makeshift tables in parking lots, while others occupy permanent stalls set up for the purpose of a market. Farmers' markets provide a place where consumers can purchase products locally, support farmers and small businesses and ultimately help the local economy.

Not just a place to shop, farmers' markets can be social affairs. Special occasions and fundraisers make the market even more festive at times, bringing more people, music and activities.

The Toledo Farmers' Market offers several events throughout the year. Often, there are cooking demonstrations, fundraisers and cooking competitions, along with live music on select days.

John Heckman, Maynard Ludwick, George Ackerman, unidentified, Ed Burr and Ed Ramasocke busy working at the Ackerman Family Farm. *Courtesy of the Ackerman family.*

At the farmers' market, it is possible to talk directly to the farmers and ask questions. Vendors are willing to share information about how their products are made and how their produce is grown and offer tips on how to use and prepare what they sell. It is not unusual to find three generations selling side by side. Young grandchildren practice their math skills, adding in their heads and counting back change.

The Toledo Farmers' Market is diverse. There are vegetables, fruits, herbs, spices and sauces, meats, honey, eggs, soap, candles, breads and baked goods and handcrafted items. The local produce is of exceptional quality, having traveled fewer miles and been picked at the right time for the best flavor. Currently, the Toledo Farmers' Market rents out 128 stalls and has approximately sixty-one vendors. Anywhere from two thousand to five thousand visitors can be expected each Saturday during the peak season.

With the increased interest in farmers' markets, several other markets have made an appearance in the Greater Toledo area. Along with the Toledo Farmers' Market in downtown Toledo, there are markets at Westgate, Perrysburg, Sylvania, Waterville and Ottawa Hills.

The Way of the Farmer

The passive American consumer, sitting down to a meal of pre-prepared or fast food, confronts a platter covered with inert, anonymous substances that have been processed, dyed, breaded, sauced, gravied, ground, pulped, strained, blended, prettified, and sanitized beyond resemblance to any part of any creature that ever lived. The products of nature and agriculture have been made, to all appearances, the products of industry.
—*Wendell Berry*

Historically, the food people ate was almost entirely regional. When Toledo was founded, settlers depended on farming, fishing, hunting and trading to obtain a variety of food items. Approximately 80 percent of Americans lived on farms in 1850, and many of those families butchered their own animals and preserved food to take them through the cold season. They knew how to prepare gardens and tend them and how to pickle, dry, smoke and can foods. Surplus was traded or sold to stores and butcher shops. Most families knew how to preserve much of their food, and tools of the time made preparation at home possible.

Those in the city were not isolated from farms. In 1919, one in four Americans still lived on farms and raised enough food to feed an additional twelve people. Farmers' markets were set up in cities, offering fresh produce to shoppers, including grocery store owners, restaurant owners and hucksters who bought produce to resell in certain areas of the city. Ice and milk were delivered, and bakeries and butcher shops were spread throughout the city, allowing people access to wholesome baked goods and fresh meats. Local shop owners often knew customers by name. In her book

This 1950s photo shows the current location of the Ackerman Berry Farm in Oregon, Ohio. *Courtesy of the Ackerman family.*

Earl, Leo and Ernest Jeffers (seated) have their wagon loaded with produce. *Courtesy of Judy Peper.*

Approximately 80 percent of Americans lived on farms in 1850, and many of those families butchered their own animals and preserved food to take them through the cold season. *Courtesy of the Ackerman family.*

In 1919, one in four Americans still lived on farms and raised enough food to feed an additional twelve people. *Courtesy of the Ackerman family.*

Jake Pound, Alfred Harringhousen, George R. Ackerman and Harold Ackerman cutting wood at the Ackerman Family Farm. *Courtesy of the Ackerman family.*

Growing Up with Featherbeds, Kerosene Lamps, and Potbelly Stoves, Doris Eggleston remembered the butcher shop well. "The butcher cut what the customer wanted, wrapped it in brown paper…Oftentimes he included a free bone for the dogs," she wrote.

In 1916, the first Piggly Wiggly opened in America and changed the way people shopped for their food. A 1924 Piggly Wiggly ad read, "Because she's sensible, knows she can save over 20% and get quality. In hot weather she likes to select personally her olives, pickles, canned and fresh fruit, sandwich delicacies, etc." No longer were foods kept behind the counter, and clerks were no longer needed to retrieve them off the shelves for customers. As the years went by, grocery stores continued to grow in size, and in 1937, the shopping cart on wheels was introduced.[5]

Not all people were pleased with one-stop grocery stores where meat was precut, packaged and displayed in coolers. "Griping about the meat counter was…common—the meat was cut too thick, too thin; there was too much or too little in a package. They wanted to watch the butcher cut the meat on a… block," Doris Eggleston wrote.[6] Despite the complaints, most people seemed pleased with the chance to buy groceries from one place because they found it convenient. And for the first time, people found it more economical to buy their milk and eggs from the store. Even though families could can and preserve vegetables and fruits over the winter, they had the option to purchase canned goods at the store. Soon, convenience won out, and many families

Max Jeffers stands with cabbages in his arms in front of a loaded truck in November 1943. On August 29, 1941, Max wrote home to his parents, "I went to market with a fifty dollar load and brought home $40…[cabbage] slowed up at 50 cents and 60 cents a bushel." *Courtesy of Judy Peper.*

The changes in food manufacturing pushed some farmers off the farm. And with the drudgery of farm life and farm chores—animals, gardens and crops to tend—children of farmers left home seeking other job opportunities. Many of them grew up with animals and gardens to tend and found leaving the responsibilities of the farm freeing. *Painting by Annette Fink.*

became reliant on weekly shopping trips. As larger chain grocery stores opened in many cities, they replaced the small mom and pop establishments, forcing owners to find other jobs. Congresswoman Marcy Kaptur's parents owned a small grocery in the Toledo area, and she remembers how they struggled with the growing competition. Marcy's father prided himself on finding quality foods from local farmers and producers and frequented the Toledo Farmers' Market. However, pressure from the large supermarkets eventually forced him to close his business.

Advancements in transportation also affected food production. Completed in 1825, the Erie Canal provided western grain growers access to urban markets on the eastern seaboard and the opportunity to export their products to Europe. By 1850, railroad lines operated as far west as the Mississippi, and by 1870, a person could take the railroad all the way to the Pacific coast. With the advent of refrigerated railroad cars, food was no longer limited by climates and seasons. Midwestern cities, such as Chicago and Kansas City, became slaughtering centers, and states became known for what they could transport. This gave people everywhere the opportunity to eat Georgia peaches, Washington and Oregon apples and Florida citrus. New England and the Middle Atlantic states became highly specialized in products such as dairy, fruits and wine.[7]

In the 1950s, refrigerators for home use became cheaper. With that and the availability of television sets, frozen TV dinners quickly followed. Advertisers claimed their frozen dinners offered a quick and easy way to prepare meals and touted the fact that everyone in the family could have what they wanted to eat. Drive-in restaurants and fast food establishments continued to multiply all over the country. By the end of the decade, more workers were processing, transporting and distributing food than were producing it on the farm, and by the 1970s, consumers paid two-thirds of every dollar for marketing costs—shipping, processing, packaging and retail.

Technological advancements in farm equipment also played a role in changing the American farm. What began as equipment pulled by horses, such as the corn binder, was eventually replaced with equipment pulled by tractors. With tractors, farmers no longer needed to keep horses or grow food for the horses and could use that land for additional crops. Today, there are specialized machines that plow, seed, harvest and thresh.[8] There are even machines that can harvest tender fruits and vegetables. The machines are expensive and complex, but these specialized machines save many hours of work. It took 373 hours in 1800 to harvest and thresh one hundred bushels of wheat and 100 hours in 1900. Just seventy years later,

Technological advancements in farm equipment also played a role in changing the American farm. *Courtesy of the Ackerman family.*

it took only 9 hours with a high-tech combine to harvest and thresh one hundred bushels of wheat.

After the mid-1950s, there were corporate mergers among grain firms, meatpacking plants, food processers and manufacturers.[9] The number of individual farms dwindled while the size of farms grew. Farms were becoming more specialized and commercialized. It was no longer profitable to raise everything on the farm. Many farmers no longer took care of animals and bought what they needed to eat at a grocery store. Farmers tended acre after acre of one or two crops that were harvested and taken away to be processed into other food items. Some farmers took out large loans in order to acquire more and more land to expand their crops and purchase expensive, specialized equipment. In the 1980s, many farm families suffered foreclosures, and the 1990s ushered in several consolidations in the food processing industry. Farmers who stayed in business had to grow more and more to keep ahead. Many signed contracts that kept them at the mercy of big businesses. Many farmers essentially became "land-owning serfs in an agricultural feudal system."[10]

Several other factors play into the change of farms and food production: selective breeding; genetically modified crops; the increased usage of synthetic pesticides; manufacturing advancements, such as new grain mills and machines that could slice and wrap; scientific discoveries, such as isolating vitamins;

George Ackerman hauling steers. *Courtesy of the Ackerman family.*

George Schmittuz used a small seeder to sow lettuce, green beans and more on his twelve-acre farm until he was in his early nineties. The seeder could be adjusted to accommodate different sizes of seeds. *Courtesy of George Dabrunz.*

Elsie Ackerman helped on the farm and at the market and cooked five meals a day for the entire farm crew. Her oldest daughter came home from school one day upset that others were saying her family was rich because they always had so much food. Elsie responded, "You just tell them that our money grows on trees and they are more than welcome to come and help us pick it." *Courtesy of the Ackerman family.*

George Dabrunz picks okra to be sold at the Toledo Farmers' Market. *Courtesy of George Dabrunz.*

It is estimated that about one-third of the human diet comes from insect-pollinated plants. The honeybee is responsible for 80 percent of that pollination. *Courtesy of Debbie Wines.*

and, of course, government regulations and policies, such as the Farm Bill. Genetically modified crops have been grown on a large commercial scale since 1996.[11] Additionally, although synthetic pesticides were used as early as the 1920s, by the 1950s, their use had become widespread.[12] The Farm Bill, an extremely complex and confusing piece of legislation, has been affecting farmers since the 1930s and is reviewed approximately every five years.

Many of the farmers at the Toledo Farmers' Market still do a lot of their own planting and harvesting, laboring from sunrise to sunset, using their family tractors and horses. They are concerned about the quality of the land and the health of their animals. Animals raised for consumption are raised humanely and without unnecessary medications or hormones. These animals get plenty of time outdoors and healthy food, unlike the majority of their cousins raised in factory farms. Much of the local meat is processed at small, nearby plants that take their time with each job.

Toledo Farmers' Market History

It is believed the Toledo Farmers' Market began in 1832, when area farmers needed a centralized place to sell their produce.[13] The market was located on Monroe, Superior and Washington Streets, which in later years became easily accessible via streetcar line. "In those old days, when the farmer arrived with his produce, he would take his team up to Billy Fieldler's feed lot. It cost 15 cents to keep and feed the horse for an entire day," Ralph E. Phelps noted in a *Toledo Blade* article in 1956.[14]

With the railroad facilities, Toledo became an "ideal distributing point for perishable produce." Farmers found the soil in the area perfect for raising vegetables and fruits, and some built hothouses to raise produce year-round for foreign markets. The demand for fresh produce was greater than the supply, and the market was always crowded, causing "intolerable traffic congestion." Vendors would often not bother with retail trade, and the city decided to create a market "to satisfy everybody." A large tract of land was purchased near Erie Street and Short Street, which was later named Market Street.[15]

In 1913, the outdoor wholesale market on Superior Street moved inside a new building constructed on Erie Street. Mention of the market in 1912 and 1913 reveals that the market was, up to that time, used almost exclusively by wholesale houses that bought in large quantities directly from the gardeners and truck farmers. Hucksters and retail dealers also purchased a considerable amount. However, with the new building, it was thought that the individual citizens would have greater interest in purchasing straight from the growers themselves.[16] Expenses of the market included pay to the laborers, who did

The market on Superior Street in 1888.

Josh Main's family has been involved in farmers' markets since 1906. This photograph shows Ernest Dewese, Josh's great-grandfather, with a wagonload of melons ready for the Weston market. Josh continues the family's farming tradition by selling at the Toledo Farmers' Market. *Courtesy of Main Creek Farms.*

This circa 1900 postcard shows the market located on Superior Street. *Courtesy of the Toledo-Lucas County Public Library.*

the cleaning, and the market master, who managed the market. In 1913, the market master received a salary of $720 a year.[17]

The outdoor market on Superior reopened in the 1910s as a retail market so that families could buy produce directly from the farmers. In addition, a retail market on Speilbusch Avenue was built in 1917. The new market, considered the "city's original curb market," had covered stalls to which vendors could easily back up with their loaded trucks. For the next several years, it appeared that the markets operated simultaneously, each being identified by its location.[18] However, the new retail market on Superior began with a rocky start when hucksters and grocers, who normally shopped at the wholesale market, started buying up all of the produce early, before shoppers arrived. In the *Toledo Blade* on July 12, 1913, it was announced that the Housewives' League wanted the city to enforce a market ordinance that made it "unlawful for anyone to purchase in the Superior Street market produce before 11 a.m. of any market day for the purpose of reselling."[19] Two days later, the *Blade* noted that the Housewives' League won its dispute, and the city council voted to prohibit street vendors from purchasing their produce at the retail farmers' market.[20]

Sometime between 1918 and 1919, part of Swan Creek was filled in, and in 1928, the building on Erie Street was remodeled to function not only as an indoor wholesale market but also as an exhibition hall and civic auditorium.[21] The remodeled building was ready by October 1929.

The Speilbusch Market, pictured here, was moved to Orange and Ontario Streets due to the construction of the new federal building in 1930. A fire raged through the Armory, the large building in the background, on December 21, 1934. *Courtesy of the Toledo-Lucas County Public Library.*

Small mom-and-pop grocery stores and local restaurants purchased goods from the vendors and farmers at the market. It was not uncommon for families to shop at the Toledo Farmers' Market to buy bushels of corn, beans, peaches, potatoes and other produce to can for the winter. *Courtesy of Eleanor Billau.*

Rachel Stanton, a member of the Sylvania Area Historical Society, remembered helping her grandfather sell at the Toledo Farmers' Market during the summer in the early 1930s. Her family lived next to her grandparents, so when school was out, she and her brother, Bud, helped them in the garden. She remembered going to bed early so that they could make it to the market by 5:00 a.m. Her grandfather had a 1929 two-door, robin egg blue Overland Whippet, and he loaded the trunk and backseat full of produce. Early in the summer, their produce included strawberries and asparagus. Later in the summer, they picked red and black raspberries, cherries and peaches.

"At the market entrance we paid the one dollar entrance fee and parked at one of the spaces marked for a farmer's vehicle," Stanton wrote. "When the market bell sounded the hucksters rushed in to buy choice produce to sell to their customers."

Stanton explained that some hucksters during that time still used horses and wagons to deliver produce, but there were others who had small delivery trucks. "They slowly drove up and down the Toledo streets shouting their available stock for the day and the residents would come to the load of fresh farm fruits and veggies," Stanton continued.

In 1930, the retail market on Speilbusch moved to Orange and Ontario Streets due to the construction of the new federal building. By 1937, Toledo boasted three municipal markets. The Erie Street Market catered

Charles Billau started helping his father at the Toledo Farmers' Market in 1938, when he was just ten years old. He continued to sell at the market until his death in 2009. *Courtesy of Eleanor Billau.*

to wholesalers, while the Speilbusch Avenue Market, at its new location on Orange and Ontario Streets, and the Berry Street Market in East Toledo—commonly known as curb markets—were set up for retail sales. "During 1936, the Erie Street Market produced $15,555 in revenue, while the operating cost was only $8,900."[22]

In 1939, Esther Gorsuch "took the Civil Service Commission examination for assistant superintendent of the Toledo Retail Markets." Esther was hired to supervise the Speilbusch Market and the smaller market on Berry Street in East Toledo. "The markets were open from 6 in the morning until 6 at night from April 1 to December 1. Esther's day started at 5:30 a.m. She walked through the stalls, checked the produce and displays, collected fees, kept records and did the books…[The farmers] came from Ohio, Michigan and Indiana, many of them returned every year."[23] Mrs. Gorsuch held her superintendent position for twenty-five years, until her retirement in 1963.

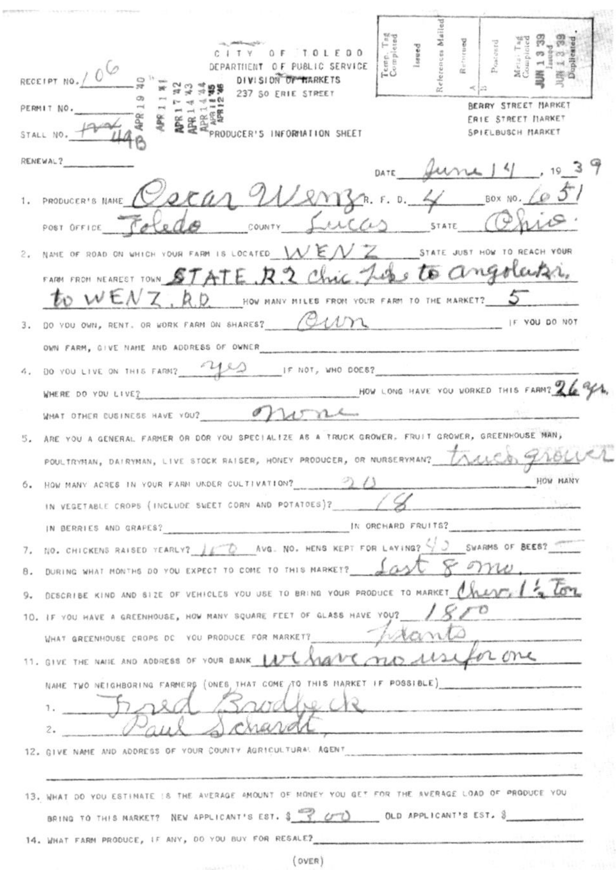

CITY OF TOLEDO
DEPARTMENT OF PUBLIC SERVICE
DIVISION OF MARKETS
237 SO ERIE STREET

PRODUCER'S INFORMATION SHEET

BERRY STREET MARKET
ERIE STREET MARKET
SPIELBUSCH MARKET

RECEIPT NO. 106
PERMIT NO. ___
STALL NO. 44B
RENEWAL? ___

DATE June 14, 1939

1. PRODUCER'S NAME Oscar Wenz R. F. D. 4 BOX NO. 651
POST OFFICE Toledo COUNTY Lucas STATE Ohio.
2. NAME OF ROAD ON WHICH YOUR FARM IS LOCATED WENZ STATE JUST HOW TO REACH YOUR FARM FROM NEAREST TOWN STATE R.2 Chic. Pike to angola Rd. to WENZ RD. HOW MANY MILES FROM YOUR FARM TO THE MARKET? 5
3. DO YOU OWN, RENT, OR WORK FARM ON SHARES? Own IF YOU DO NOT OWN FARM, GIVE NAME AND ADDRESS OF OWNER ___
4. DO YOU LIVE ON THIS FARM? yes IF NOT, WHO DOES? ___
WHERE DO YOU LIVE? ___ HOW LONG HAVE YOU WORKED THIS FARM? 26 yr.
WHAT OTHER BUSINESS HAVE YOU? None
5. ARE YOU A GENERAL FARMER OR DO YOU SPECIALIZE AS A TRUCK GROWER, FRUIT GROWER, GREENHOUSE MAN, POULTRYMAN, DAIRYMAN, LIVE STOCK RAISER, HONEY PRODUCER, OR NURSERYMAN? truck grower
6. HOW MANY ACRES IN YOUR FARM UNDER CULTIVATION? 20 HOW MANY IN VEGETABLE CROPS (INCLUDE SWEET CORN AND POTATOES)? 18
IN BERRIES AND GRAPES? ___ IN ORCHARD FRUITS? ___
7. NO. CHICKENS RAISED YEARLY? 100 AVG. NO. HENS KEPT FOR LAYING? 40 SWARMS OF BEES? —
8. DURING WHAT MONTHS DO YOU EXPECT TO COME TO THIS MARKET? Last 8 mo.
9. DESCRIBE KIND AND SIZE OF VEHICLES YOU USE TO BRING YOUR PRODUCE TO MARKET Chev. 1½ Ton
10. IF YOU HAVE A GREENHOUSE, HOW MANY SQUARE FEET OF GLASS HAVE YOU? 1800
WHAT GREENHOUSE CROPS DO YOU PRODUCE FOR MARKET? Plants
11. GIVE THE NAME AND ADDRESS OF YOUR BANK we have no use for one
NAME TWO NEIGHBORING FARMERS (ONES THAT COME TO THIS MARKET IF POSSIBLE)
1. Fred Brodbeck
2. Paul Schardt
12. GIVE NAME AND ADDRESS OF YOUR COUNTY AGRICULTURAL AGENT ___
13. WHAT DO YOU ESTIMATE IS THE AVERAGE AMOUNT OF MONEY YOU GET FOR THE AVERAGE LOAD OF PRODUCE YOU BRING TO THIS MARKET? NEW APPLICANT'S EST. $ 900 OLD APPLICANT'S EST. $ ___
14. WHAT FARM PRODUCE, IF ANY, DO YOU BUY FOR RESALE? ___

(OVER)

Extensive applications were required of the vendors between 1939 and 1975. An amazing amount of information can be gleaned from the surviving applications. *Courtesy of the Toledo Farmers' Market Association.*

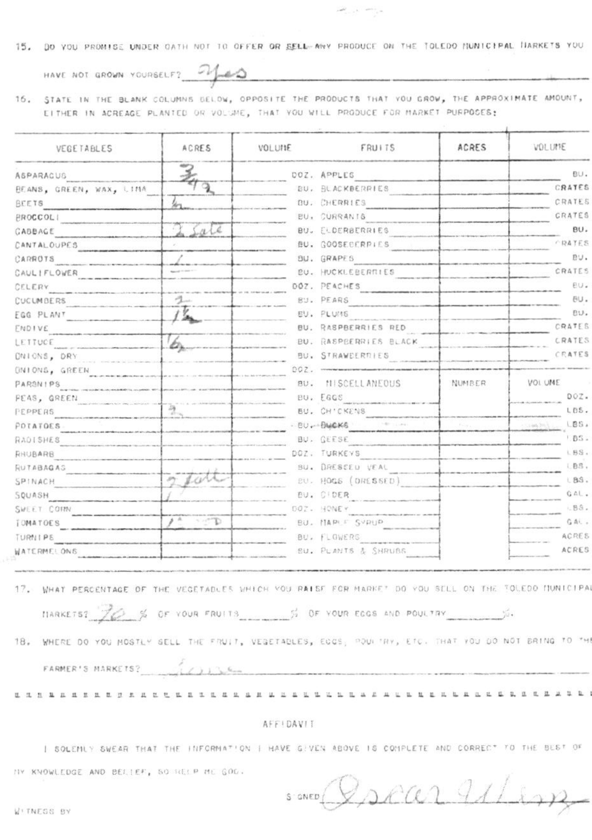

15. DO YOU PROMISE UNDER OATH NOT TO OFFER OR SELL ANY PRODUCE ON THE TOLEDO MUNICIPAL MARKETS YOU HAVE NOT GROWN YOURSELF? Yes

16. STATE IN THE BLANK COLUMNS BELOW, OPPOSITE THE PRODUCTS THAT YOU GROW, THE APPROXIMATE AMOUNT, EITHER IN ACREAGE PLANTED OR VOLUME, THAT YOU WILL PRODUCE FOR MARKET PURPOSES:

VEGETABLES	ACRES	VOLUME	FRUITS	ACRES	VOLUME
ASPARAGUS	¾	DOZ.	APPLES		BU.
BEANS, GREEN, WAX, LIMA	½	BU.	BLACKBERRIES		CRATES
BEETS	½	BU.	CHERRIES		CRATES
BROCCOLI		BU.	CURRANTS		CRATES
CABBAGE	2 Sale	BU.	ELDERBERRIES		BU.
CANTALOUPES		BU.	GOOSEBERRIES		CRATES
CARROTS	1	BU.	GRAPES		BU.
CAULIFLOWER	—	BU.	HUCKLEBERRIES		CRATES
CELERY		DOZ.	PEACHES		BU.
CUCUMBERS	2	BU.	PEARS		BU.
EGG PLANT	1½	BU.	PLUMS		BU.
ENDIVE		BU.	RASPBERRIES RED		CRATES
LETTUCE	½	BU.	RASPBERRIES BLACK		CRATES
ONIONS, DRY		BU.	STRAWBERRIES		CRATES
ONIONS, GREEN		DOZ.			
PARSNIPS		BU.	MISCELLANEOUS	NUMBER	VOLUME
PEAS, GREEN		BU.	EGGS		DOZ.
PEPPERS	2	BU.	CHICKENS		LBS.
POTATOES		BU.	DUCKS		LBS.
RADISHES		BU.	GEESE		LBS.
RHUBARB		DOZ.	TURKEYS		LBS.
RUTABAGAS		BU.	DRESSED VEAL		LBS.
SPINACH	2 fall	BU.	HOGS (DRESSED)		LBS.
SQUASH		BU.	CIDER		GAL.
SWEET CORN		DOZ.	HONEY		LBS.
TOMATOES	1½ [illegible]	BU.	MAPLE SYRUP		GAL.
TURNIPS		BU.	FLOWERS		ACRES
WATERMELONS		BU.	PLANTS & SHRUBS		ACRES

17. WHAT PERCENTAGE OF THE VEGETABLES WHICH YOU RAISE FOR MARKET DO YOU SELL ON THE TOLEDO MUNICIPAL MARKETS? 70 % OF YOUR FRUITS ____ % OF YOUR EGGS AND POULTRY ____ %.

18. WHERE DO YOU MOSTLY SELL THE FRUIT, VEGETABLES, EGGS, POULTRY, ETC. THAT YOU DO NOT BRING TO THE FARMER'S MARKETS? None

AFFIDAVIT

I SOLEMNLY SWEAR THAT THE INFORMATION I HAVE GIVEN ABOVE IS COMPLETE AND CORRECT TO THE BEST OF MY KNOWLEDGE AND BELIEF, SO HELP ME GOD.

SIGNED Oscar Wenz

WITNESS BY

The back of the farmers' market applications included an area where vendors were asked to list the total amount of acreage they dedicated to each crop. *Courtesy of the Toledo Farmers' Market Association.*

Between 1939 and 1975, extensive applications were required of the vendors. Some old files include references from neighbors and others recommending the applicant and considering him to have a good reputation. An amazing amount of information can be gleaned from the surviving applications. Questions included acreage farmed and how many years they farmed the land, the kind of vehicle they drove to the market and the estimated amount of money they got for the load of produce they brought to market. Answers revealed if they held other jobs or had fruit trees on their land and how many hens they kept for egg production. In 1939, applications asked for the name and address of the vendor's bank. In reply to the inquiry of which bank they used, farmer Oscar Wenz wrote, "We have no use for one."

In 1940, the Spielbusch retail market moved to the outdoor area at the back of the Erie Street building. The market hosted more than two hundred vendors, selling on Tuesday, Thursday and Saturday. The first row of stalls was considered Wholesale Row because once the inside wholesale market closed for the day, wholesalers came out and sold at Wholesale Row. Vendors sold poultry and eggs in the back row of stalls, close to Swan Creek. Saturday was always a busy day at the market. Small mom and pop grocery stores and local restaurants purchased goods from the vendors and farmers. It was not uncommon for families to shop at the Toledo Farmers' Market and buy bushels of corn, beans, peaches, potatoes and other produce to can for the winter.

Larry Wagner, who grew up on a farm near Holland, remembered working alongside his father, grandfather and great-grandfather throughout the summers. Following the tractor and attached potato digger, Larry picked up the potatoes and placed them in bushel baskets. When all the potatoes were in baskets, Larry's father pulled the wagon along the rows, and the bushel baskets were loaded and stacked carefully. Once in the barn, the potatoes were graded by size, weighed and bagged. They sold the potatoes directly from the farm or hauled them to the Toledo Farmers' Market to be sold. Larry's grandfather picked him up at four o'clock in the morning, and they would stop at Clara's Restaurant for breakfast before the market started.[24]

The Billau family harvested potatoes to sell for many years. *Courtesy of Eleanor Billau.*

In their family barn, Eleanor Billau grades potatoes by size. *Courtesy of Eleanor Billau.*

Clara's Restaurant, in the corner building at 626 Market Street, was a popular stop for some vendors. Starting in 1943, the Godfreys served up breakfast and lunch at Clara's Restaurant for approximately forty years.[25] "What wonderful pancakes and bacon that place served," Larry Wagner remembered.[26] Clara Godfrey, for whom the restaurant was named, ran the restaurant with help from her family. The restaurant was well known for its hearty portions and Clara's homemade pies. Every morning, the Godfreys arrived before the market to get things ready for predawn customers. Clara, who learned how to cook from her Polish mother, made six to eight pies a day.[27]

New health code regulations were enacted by the City Health Department, and by June 1961, there were empty stalls throughout the Toledo Farmers' Market. The new code read: "Under no circumstance shall any processed food or food product be displayed or sold upon the market. This shall include dressed chickens, baked goods, home canned goods, cheese, etc."[28] Health regulations drove away several sellers and their home-processed goods, including a lady from Michigan who brought home-baked cakes and cookies and a woman with home-canned preserves and jellies. Baked goods and preserves could no longer be made at home; they had to be made in a licensed and inspected kitchen.[29]

By mid-August 1962, farmers could see that business was not as it used to be. The outdoor market was open each Tuesday, Thursday and Saturday

George Schmittuz and his wife, Lily, took special care with their plants. In their greenhouse, they tended to tuberous begonias. *Courtesy of George Dabrunz.*

Evelyn Harms (née Jeffers), Mildred Brown (née Carter) and Marjorie Thomas (née Jennings) stand in front of a wagon loaded with gladiolas from Jeffers Gardens. *Courtesy of Judy Peper.*

at six o'clock in the morning. Although the stalls were required to close by six o'clock in the evening, few vendors stayed past the early afternoon. Some vendors found Tuesdays and Thursdays difficult days to sell and often did not make enough money to cover the price of gasoline for the drive to the market. Saturday remained the best day for selling. Those who sold at the market paid a rental fee of $27.50 per stall during the growing season, running from May 1 to November 30. Corner stalls were rented for $35.00.[30]

During the mid-1960s, business at the market was declining. Many families were no longer canning food and found shopping at large supermarkets more convenient. In 1966, the wholesale market was moved out of the building on Erie Street so that the city could use the building as a garage and storage.

In the fall of 1970, there were eighty-three farmers renting stalls. For the season from May 1 to November 30, they paid seventy dollars for six-day rentals and forty dollars for three days a week. Those who sold daily paid a two-dollar daily fee.[31]

By mid-November 1970, the city administration announced it would not be opening the market in the spring of 1971. William Veasey, commissioner of public buildings, explained that the revenue from the market operations, including fees for use of truck scales and stall rent, had slowly decreased over the last three years. He added that the city needed additional space for storing vehicles and equipment. The city proposed moving the market to nine acres of city-owned land on Hill Avenue near Elmdale Road. It suggested the city could lease the land to the farmers and that the farmers would pay for the development and maintenance. The city estimated the cost of development to be $240,000.

By this time, many vendors had begun their plans for the following year. The announcement was a surprise and was met with opposition. Many felt that the eighty-three vendors who were currently renting the stalls should have been consulted before the decision was made. Vendors and shoppers expressed their views to the council, claiming that the Hill Avenue location could not be reached by public transportation and it would hurt low-income families who shopped at the market. The farmers collected signatures opposing such a move, and they showed up at council meetings. At one council meeting, city manager William Gross halted the market's move following protests. Gross explained that the plan had originated because of the need for storage and parking space for city divisions in the old civic auditorium. In response, Adella Hanselman, speaking on behalf of the farmers, asked, "Why don't you put your cotton-pickin' stuff in the boondocks?"[32] Harold Shelt, treasurer of the Farmers' Market Association, proposed increasing stall rental fees to help with the increased costs of managing the market. The Farmers' Market brought in $8,318 but had expenses of $15,041 in 1970. By raising rates in 1971, the Farmers' Market could possibly pay for itself for the first time in three years.[33]

By December, vice mayor Harry W. Kessler, a member of the business and industry committee, initiated a proposal to raise rates and keep the market open for another year, allowing the city to resolve its space problems. Even with the increase of revenue from the market, C.E. Riser, commissioner of traffic engineering, still supported closing the market due to the animosity between farmers and city employees concerning the limited number of parking spaces. The limitations on parking prompted embarrassing fights from both the city employees and farmers when city employees parked in the Toledo Farmers' Market lot instead of the lot provided for them on the south side of the building. A letter from C.E. Riser cited episodes of egg and tomato throwing and an incidence of a city employee throwing away the keys to a farmer's vehicle.[34]

The voices of the farmers and business and industry committee were heard, and the council decided to keep the Toledo Farmers' Market at its location through 1971. Rates for stall rental were increased to a seasonal fee of $115 and $125 for corner and poultry stalls. Under the new agreement, the city could rent out a stall for the day if it were not occupied by 6:30 a.m. Daily rates were increased to $3 a day on weekdays and $5 on Saturdays.[35] The increase of rates was discouraging, especially to the small-scale vendors who sold at the market. Some felt the increase would drive smaller producers away and affect the pricing on the products being sold at the market.[36]

In 1973, the market master, Al Bodi, said that farmers were "doing a little better than last year." He estimated that Saturdays brought in more than five thousand visitors. Area farmers brought in ninety-three loads of produce, and all 143 stalls were in operation. Mr. Bodi figured the main selling points for the produce at the market were the variety and selection available.[37]

Business at the market had changed quite a bit since World War II. "People have changed their eating and buying habits," Lyle Romstadt of Curtice told the *Toledo Blade*. He had seen the ups and down of the market, having worked the market since he was a child. "They don't need to come here when they can buy tomatoes [at the grocery store]...year round," he continued.[38]

Mrs. Walter Homan sold dressed chickens at the market and was often asked for advice on how to fry chicken by new customers. "It's surprising

Right: This 1973 list was found among several log books in the market's collection that survived through the years. *Courtesy of the Toledo Farmers' Market Association.*

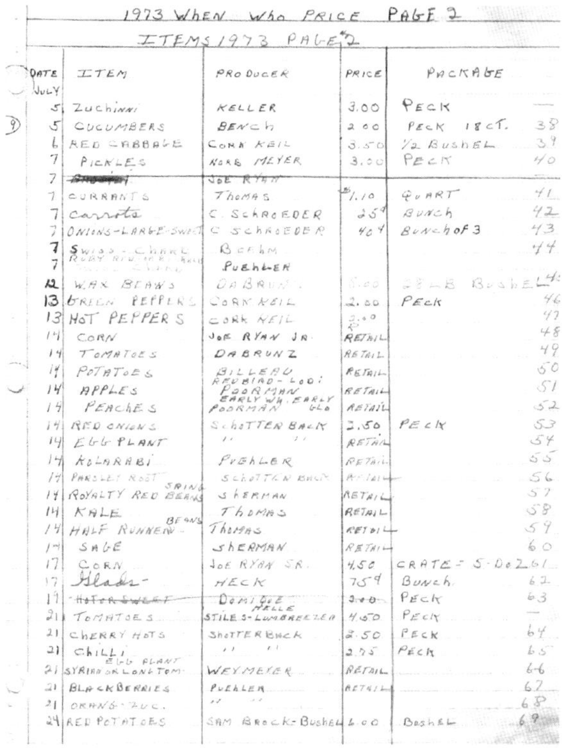

1973 WHEN WHO PRICE PAGE 2

ITEMS 1973 PAGE #2

DATE JULY	ITEM	PRODUCER	PRICE	PACKAGE	
5	ZUCHINNI	KELLER	3.00	PECK	—
5	CUCUMBERS	BENCH	2.00	PECK 18 CT.	38
6	RED CABBAGE	CORN KEIL	3.50	½ BUSHEL	39
7	PICKLES	NORB MEYER	3.00	PECK	40
7	~~[illegible]~~	JOE RYAN			
7	CURRANTS	THOMAS	$1.10	QUART	41
7	Carrots	C. SCHROEDER	25¢	BUNCH	42
7	ONIONS-LARGE-SWEET	C SCHROEDER	40¢	BUNCH OF 3	43
7	SWISS CHARD	BOEHM			44
7	RUBY [illegible]	PUEHLER			
12	WAX BEANS	DABRUNZ	[illegible]	[illegible] LB BUSHEL	45
13	GREEN PEPPERS	CORN KEIL	2.00	PECK	46
13	HOT PEPPERS	CORN KEIL	2.00 R		47
14	CORN	JOE RYAN JR.	RETAIL		48
14	TOMATOES	DABRUNZ	RETAIL		49
14	POTATOES	BILLEAU	RETAIL		50
14	APPLES	RED BIRD - LODI: POORMAN	RETAIL		51
14	PEACHES	EARLY WH. EARLY GLO POORMAN	RETAIL		52
14	RED ONIONS	SCHOTTENBACK	2.50	PECK	53
14	EGG PLANT	" "	RETAIL		54
14	KOLARABI	PUEHLER	RETAIL		55
14	PARSLEY ROOT	SCHOTTENBACK	RETAIL		56
14	ROYALTY RED STRING BEANS	SHERMAN	RETAIL		57
14	KALE	THOMAS	RETAIL		58
14	HALF RUNNER BEANS	Thomas	RETAIL		59
14	SAGE	SHERMAN	RETAIL		60
17	CORN	JOE RYAN SR.	4.50	CRATE - 5 - DOZ	61
17	Glads -	HECK	75¢	BUNCH	62
19	~~HOT OR SWEET~~	DOMIQUE	3.00	PECK	63
21	TOMATOES	STILES - LUMBREEZER MELLE	4.50	PECK	—
21	CHERRY HOTS	SHOTTERBACK	2.50	PECK	64
21	CHILLI	" "	2.75	PECK	65
21	EGG PLANT SYRIAN OR LONG TOM	WEYMEYER	RETAIL		66
21	BLACKBERRIES	PUEHLER	RETAIL		67
21	ORANG ZUC.	" "			68
24	RED POTATOES	SAM BROCK - BUSHEL	6.00	BUSHEL	69

Below: Several log books in the market's collection have survived through the years. These books include names, stall rental fees and how much was collected.

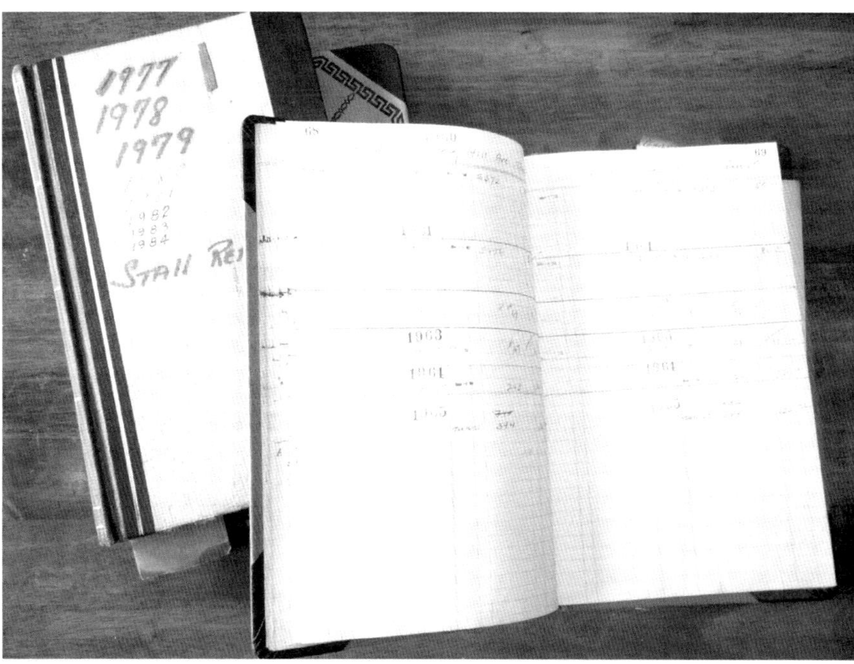

This photograph, taken in 1974, shows how the boxes and crates were stored on the low roofs of the stalls. *Courtesy of Eleanor Billau.*

how many people nowadays don't know how to cook," Homan told the *Toledo Blade*. Up until the early 1960s, she sold live chickens. Some people can remember going to the market when live chickens were sold. The chickens were placed upside down in a bag, with their heads poking out of little holes. This subdued the chicken while the customer took it home. Most of the chickens sold this way were killed and butchered at home. However, by the 1970s, this practice had fallen out of favor, and consumers wanted to buy their meat out of grocery store refrigerators—chickens already killed, cleaned and packaged.[39]

In 1980, the *Toledo Blade* Living Today section included articles on preserving food, and many recipes featured items that could be purchased at the Toledo Farmers' Market. Readers learned how to shop for melons and how to can tomatoes. In mid-August, food editor Mary Alice Powell wrote that the Toledo Farmers' Market was "fragrant with dill, lush with leaf lettuce and turnip and mustard greens, and bright with plums and sweet corn."[40]

In this photograph, Clifford Myers, better known as "Red Hot," and his helper go through their produce. Red Hot sold turnips, cabbage, potatoes, yams, mustard greens, Brussels sprouts, watermelons and red hot peppers. He could be heard throughout the market yelling, "Red hot, get 'em red hot!" *Courtesy of Eleanor Billau.*

Oscar, standing next to a produce scale, was a huckster many remember. Oscar would visit the market and buy choice produce to resell in Toledo. *Courtesy of Eleanor Billau.*

This photograph, taken in 1987, shows how much produce was brought in by each vendor. Some vendors who have been farming and selling at the market for many years can remember when they hauled in up to three truckloads every Saturday. *Courtesy of Eleanor Billau.*

In 1985, the Toledo Farmers' Market incurred an operating deficit of $4,227. Winter stall rent was considered for an increase from $190 to $200 in order to help cover these costs. The increase seemed justified; however, there were obvious problems with the structure. The 144 stalls were in need of repair, having, over time, slowly sunken into the soft soil.[41] Older stalls at the end, near Swan Creek, had been occupied by indigents, and the deteriorated wood was vulnerable to fire damage by vandals. Along with damaged and rusty eave troughs, the roof leaked, and trash was not cleared regularly. A lack of signage also made the market hard to find.[42]

In May 1986, the market had a slow start, and the Toledo Farmers' Market Association resorted to collecting money from its members to advertise summer activities. Members were urged to contribute five dollars each. The old argument about limited parking was revisited, and there was talk about creating a corporation to lease and operate the market.[43]

That year, the Greater Toledo Marketing Group invited the Toledo Farmers' Market to participate in Market Day in the Park. A temporary market was set up at Promenade Park on August 21 to help boost awareness

Alfred Flick was a Toledo Farmers' Market vendor who participated in the Market Day at Promenade Park. The market was set up at the park temporarily on August 21, 1986, to help boost awareness of the downtown market. *Courtesy of Eleanor Billau.*

of the downtown market. Hoping to give the Toledo Farmers' Market exposure, fourteen market vendors were set up at the end of the old Edison Steam Plant from 11:00 a.m. to 6:00 p.m. that day.[44]

The market continued to face problems, and according to some, it was "being treated as an orphan." The market was still operated by the city and was, according to city officials, still running at a deficit. Stall rent was increased in 1986 from $190 to $210, yet the vendors still made do with leaky roofs, a shortage of parking for shoppers and no signage directing traffic to the market. Eli Lutife, a seventy-nine-year-old who started huckstering at the Toledo Farmers' Market in the 1930s, wished the city did more to publicize the market. "If they really want something in the downtown, they ought to knock down some of these old buildings in four square blocks and build a real market," he emphasized.[45] A new city ordinance decreed that the market be open only on Saturdays during the winter and on three days—Tuesday, Thursday and Saturday—during the summer.[46]

By 1988, the Toledo Farmers' Market had been moved under the jurisdiction of William Scalzo, director of natural resources. He was enthusiastic about rebuilding the market and upgrading the area around Swan Creek and Superior Street. Scalzo met several times with vendors to get ideas on improvements.[47]

The Billau family often gave produce to the Toledo Gospel Rescue Mission. The produce helped supply nutritious food for the meals served at the mission. *Courtesy of Eleanor Billau.*

In September, it was announced that the Toledo Plan Commission had endorsed $500,000 in improvements to the Farmers' Market in hopes it would play a role in renewing interest in the historic Warehouse District. The city council approved $50,000 for initial work, "including new signs and some new stalls, cleaning up Swan Creek, and regrading the land."[48]

Plans included new stalls that would be slightly bigger, with wide, covered walkways; public restrooms; and a new office. A wooden walkway and landscaping would be built along Swan Creek. The plans of the new market structure were drawn up; however, many of the vendors felt the new market would cost too much to build. They also believed the new design—with octagonal centers, tall roofs and lines of stalls placed close together—would allow rain to blow in from the sides and not allow easy access to stalls with large trucks.[49]

By January 1990, the first phase of the rebuilding was well underway. Fourteen new stalls of solid oak were erected by craftsmen from Riverbend Timber Framing, Inc., of Blissfield, Michigan. Mack Magee, the project coordinator for Riverbend, explained the process to the *Toledo Blade*. Mortise and tenon joints were pegged with wood dowels. The oak frames were constructed on the ground and raised by crane into position.[50] Work on thirty-three additional stalls began in 1991.[51]

The 1990s ushered in several changes for the market, including the reemergence of homemade goods. The Cottage Food Production Operation, now part of the Ohio Revised Code, permits people to produce "food items that are not potentially hazardous" in one's home. These foods include baked goods, jams, jellies, candies, fruit butters and other similar products.[52] This enabled sellers to bring these items back to the market, and new vendors with pies, jams, breads, cookies and more applied for stalls.

A 1991 study conducted by the U.S. Department of Agriculture recommended that the Toledo Farmers' Market be managed by an organization other than the city. "The city just hasn't had the time or the funds to promote the market as it should be promoted," Ross Hamre, senior park planner, told the *Toledo Blade* in March 1993. After attending

By January 1990, the first phase of the rebuilding of the Toledo Farmers' Market was well underway. *Courtesy of Eleanor Billau.*

The rebuilding of the Toledo Farmers' Market happened in stages. Everyone anticipated its completion. *Courtesy of Eleanor Billau.*

an international market conference in 1991, Hamre said, "I could not help notice that many of the farmers' markets are being managed by someone who is a zealot about the merits of shopping at their market. They see it as a cultural activity, not just an acquisition of food."[53]

Throughout 1992 and 1993, there was a lot of discussion about privatizing the Toledo Farmers' Market.[54] By the spring of 1994, the newly formed Toledo Farmers' Market Association took over the responsibilities of day-to-day market operations from the city's Department of Natural Resources. The Toledo Farmers' Market Association formed as a cooperative of vendors who sold at the market. Louise Mikesell-Wireman became the director of the association, and the officers included Ralph Keefe, Norm Keil, Anna Miller and Ron Beltz. Special events at the market in 1994 included Flower Day, a northwest Ohio Firefighters Soup-Off, Strawberry Surprise, Melon Mania, Harvest Festival and Hobo Dinner.[55] "The market is looking better than ever. There is a renewed spirit and vitality and we're excited about this upcoming year," Ralph Keefe stated in a brochure announcing the grand opening.

The official opening of the market in May that year included daylong demonstrations on flower and vegetable gardening and special appearances by Muddy the Mud Hen and Fireman Freddy. Displays included a vintage 1937 fire engine from the Toledo Fire Department Museum and an exotic petting zoo, where kids could pet an iguana. The market was busy from the time it opened at 6:00 a.m., and many of the vendors selling baked goods ran out by early afternoon.[56]

Under the Toledo Farmers' Market Association, the market was receiving more attention. A new bridge was constructed over Swan Creek, linking Superior Street and St. Clair Street. Many watched the construction move slowly with hopes that it would eventually draw more people to the downtown area.

More improvements took place during the winter of 1995 and 1996, and the new market made its debut the weekend of July 12, 1996. The gravel walks were replaced with concrete walkways, and new lighting replaced the dim light sockets. Additionally, new uniform tables lined the walkway.

The Farmers' Market Coupon Program was sponsored by congresswoman Marcy Kaptur. It was implemented in 2001 and intended to help seniors obtain more fruits and vegetables from local and independent growers. Up to $120 in coupons were distributed to northwest Ohio residents who were sixty years or older and had incomes of less than $21,000 annually. They could redeem their coupons at roadside produce stands throughout ten counties—Lucas, Fulton, Wood, Ottawa, Williams, Henry, Paulding, Erie, Defiance

Muddy the Mud Hen has been known to show up at the Toledo Farmers' Market during special events. Here is Muddy in 2001, showing a potato to children visiting the market. *Courtesy of Eleanor Billau.*

Part of the new market, as it still looks today. *Courtesy of Eleanor Billau.*

and Sandusky Counties—and at the Toledo Farmers' Market from May 1 through October 31. "This…provides an excellent opportunity for Northwest Ohio farmers to sell their products locally while assisting seniors with their nutritional needs," Kaptur emphasized in a press release in January 2001.[57]

The program generated quite a bit of interest, but unfortunately the Area Office on Aging gave out more vouchers than there were funds available. Farmers were unable to receive reimbursement for the vouchers they received until the U.S. Department of Agriculture granted a one-time supplemental payment in the amount of $400,000 to the Area Office of Aging to cover the vouchers.[58]

The senior coupon program was similar to the vouchers distributed through the Women, Infants and Children program, also known as WIC. However, it was estimated that more senior coupons were redeemed than offered through the WIC program. Seniors made it a point to get to the market, at times arriving by bus or riding with friends. Eleanor Billau remembered one lady who lived downtown arriving on her bicycle and taking her produce home in the attached basket. Some seniors were stocking up for winter—buying items they could store, like potatoes and onions; sweet corn to freeze; or tomatoes and cucumbers to can.

Several dedicated vendors continued to sell through the winter months. They brought their items to the market, and on the coldest days, they would sit in their cars to stay warm in between sales. U.S. representative Marcy Kaptur remembered going to the market in the winter and seeing the dedicated few waiting for their customers. With Kaptur's help, a $48,000 grant provided by the U.S. Department of Housing and Urban Development was procured for roll-down doors to be used in the winter months at the market.

Charles Billau in 2004. Charles Billau started helping his father at the Toledo Farmers' Market in 1938, when he was just ten years old. *Courtesy of Eleanor Billau.*

In December 2007, eight roll-down doors were installed at one section of the market's open-air building, allowing a number of vendors to sell throughout the winter on a regular basis. Six more roll-down doors were installed in 2010. Josh Main of Main Creek Farms remembers the addition of the roll-down doors well. "No more cold winter Saturdays," he writes.

The latter half of the decade also brought back a way for vendors to accept Ohio's Direction Card, the state's food stamp program. The Toledo

Anna Miller of Quarry Farm Gourds displays her dried gourd birdhouses in 2004. Anna sold at the Toledo Farmers' Market for several years and carried a variety of fresh-cut flowers, dried flowers and gourds. *Courtesy of Eleanor Billau.*

Farmers' Market also has a credit card machine for those who prefer not to carry cash.

Today, the Toledo Farmers' Market is open every Saturday year-round. During the winter, the market hosts approximately eighteen to twenty vendors. During the growing season, as many as sixty vendors sell at the market. The year 2011 marked the twenty-second annual Flower Day, a popular springtime event that draws more than fifty thousand people to the market over the three-day weekend.

The Toledo Farmers' Market has survived many tough challenges but continues to be the place to be on Saturday mornings. Toledo is blessed with a year-round farmers' market, and it is the place to go to find fresh local food. It is a place to try something new and a place to take in all the best that

Toledo is blessed with a year-round farmers' market, and it is the place to go to find fresh local food. *Courtesy of Tom and Margie Lumbrezer.*

Northwest Ohio and Southeast Michigan have to offer. The market narrows the gap between the field and the family's dinner table. What Eleanor Billau once wrote still holds true today: "We will never outgrow our need for fresh fruits, vegetables, plants, flowers, baked goods, fresh eggs, and poultry that is available at the market."

Vendors

Did you ever think how a bit of land shows the character of the owner?
—Laura Ingalls Wilder

There are over sixty vendors who currently sell at the Toledo Farmers' Market. What follows is a bit of background on many of those vendors. This is by no means a definitive list. The Toledo Farmers' Market follows the seasons, and it was difficult to gather all the stories in time to include in this book. Perhaps this book will bring more market stories to light and warrant a second edition. Although this is not a comprehensive list, it will definitely show the variety of the products offered at the market. The Toledo Farmers' Market has dedicated vendors who make up the rich market history. The Toledo Farmers' Market is always changing, so the best way to experience it is to visit often.

Ackerman Berry Farm

www.ackermanberryfarm.com

The Ackerman family emigrated from Germany to Oregon, Ohio, in the mid- to late 1800s and have been farming ever since. The Ackermans started selling at the Toledo Farmers' Market in the early 1900s and used a wagon pulled by horse to take their products to the market. They came down Corduroy Road, so named because of the logs from which it was

The Ackerman family emigrated from Germany to Oregon, Ohio, in the mid- to late 1800s and have been farming ever since. *Courtesy of the Ackerman family.*

constructed, and crossed a bridge that was located at the corner of Front and Consul Streets in Toledo.

Even though the Ackermans have grown a variety of fruits and vegetables over the years, they are best known for growing quality fruit like peaches, apples, cherries and more. At present, the Ackermans grow raspberries, blackberries, currants and gooseberries. Gary and Carolyn Ackerman, who currently sell at the market, not only have fruits available at market but also carry seedless purees, vinaigrettes and raspberry lemonade.

AMY'S CUSTOM CHOCOLATES

www.amyscustomchocolates.com

Amy Hendricks has been selling at the market since June 2010, making custom chocolates and tasty breads. Hendricks has been baking since she was a young girl. She learned from her mother, helping her in the kitchen to make cookies, cakes, quick breads, pies and candies. Hendricks started making homemade goodies for friends and family, but when others got a taste of her baked goods, they asked if they could purchase them for holidays and special occasions. Soon, she was putting together orders for people from school, church and from a local catering company. The Toledo Farmers' Market worked into her schedule and has become an outlet for her to sell her wonderful creations.

Andy Keil Greenhouse

www.andykeil.com

Andy Keil is a third-generation farmer. Some of his earliest memories include coming to the market with his father and grandfather. Today, his own grandchildren share the experience with him. Keil remembers when the market was also a wholesale market, selling produce to small grocery stores and restaurants. Some days, the Keils were at the market as early as one o'clock in the morning to prepare for the day and often made deliveries on the way home. Keil has a connection with the land and does not hesitate to pluck something up and eat it right from the field. "Farming's in my blood," he explained. Keil still fills all of his flats by hand, and everything in the field is still harvested without the aid of large equipment.

Andy Keil remembers when the market was also a wholesale market, selling to small grocery stores and restaurants.

THE BAKING BROTHERS

www.thebakingbrothers.com

The Baking Brothers consists of three brothers—Ian, Ethan and Drew Downing—who specialize in baked goods made with recipes handed down from their great-grandmother, Lilian Lapointe. Lilian was born in 1878 on a farm in Michigan and baked using whole grain flours, fresh butter and cream and fruits grown on her farm. She worked from memory, and her recipes were never written down until her daughter, the Baking Brothers' mother, recorded them in the late 1960s. Now, her grandchildren use her recipes to make the delicious baked goods they sell at the Toledo Farmers' Market. The Baking Brothers donate a percentage of all their profits to the La Posada Shelter in Toledo, which provides temporary housing to those in need.

BARROW'S GREENHOUSE

Linda Barrow, Greg's mother, helps out at both the Perrysburg Farmers' Market and the Toledo Farmers' Market.

Located on Northwood Avenue in Toledo, Barrow's Greenhouse has been growing top-quality plants since 1893. When Greg Barrow's great-grandfather started the greenhouse, it was located on Dorr Street and Detroit Avenue. Later, the family moved their business to Dorr Street and Monroe Street, across from the Swayne Field Ballpark. Another move took them to Monroe Street and Central Avenue. For many years, the greenhouse was exclusively wholesale, but with the growth of big box stores that bypass local growers, Barrow's Greenhouse has adapted to meet retail demand. The greenhouse sells houseplants year-round. It grows spring bedding plants and hardy mums in the fall, and in the winter, it supplies poinsettias.

Billau Farms

Charles Billau started going to the Toledo Farmers' market when he was just a young boy. His wife, Eleanor, still helps their youngest of three children, Mike, along with his family at the market. Not only has the Billau family been farming their 103-acre family farm in Whiteford Township, Michigan, for over 150 years, but they are also

Top: Mike Billau's wife, Debi, is shown here with her daughter, Melissa. Melissa was born on a Wednesday evening, and Debi arrived at the market that Saturday morning with newborn Melissa in tow, after being discharged from the hospital. Like Melissa and her brother Shawn, many vendors and their families can remember growing up surrounded by the market. *Courtesy of Eleanor Billau.*

Bottom: This 1980s photograph shows Charles Billau and his grandson Joel planting onion sets on his farm in Michigan. *Courtesy of Eleanor Billau.*

actively involved in their community. Mike and his son Shawn are volunteer firefighters for the Whiteford Township Fire Department and are responsible for a family tradition of digging graves for Whiteford Union Cemetery.

Blue Stem Garden, LLC

Pam Poeth of Blue Stem Gardens has been caring for plants and animals since she was a child. Both of her parents grew up on farms, and the Poeth family lived in a rural area where Pam helped her parents take care of the farm and animals. At the Toledo Farmers' Market, she sells a variety of seasonal items from her garden, including lettuce, heirloom tomatoes and cut flowers. Pam also offers several baked goods items and is known for her soft pretzels and whole grain muffins. She uses organic butter and eggs and natural sweeteners like honey and molasses in her products to make them satisfying and wholesome.

Campbell Poultry House

In addition to regular vendor stalls, the market has a poultry house in a freestanding building that is open six days a week. Jan Campbell, who runs the poultry house, has been coming to the market since she was young. Her family, the Homans, began selling live chickens, ducks and geese at the market in 1943 and began offering dressed poultry in 1967. Although Jan no longer raises her own to sell, she provides customers with Miller Amish Country Poultry and whole broilers, turkeys, Cornish hens and eggs from several different local farmers.

Canal Junction Farmstead Cheese

www.canaljunctioncheese.com

Brian Schlatter is the master cheese maker of the family owned and operated Canal Junction Farmstead Cheese. Brian comes from a family of farmers and studied cheese making at the University of Vermont. His delicious artisan cheeses are made right on the farm, where the highest-quality raw milk is used. The family raises their cows without synthetic hormones on grass that is herbicide and pesticide free.

Brian Schlatter was in 4-H as a child. Here, he shows a cow in 1996. *Courtesy of the Schlatter family.*

Corbin Schlatter, Brian's brother, stands with the family's dog. The milking barn can be seen in the background. *Courtesy of the Schlatter family.*

COUNTRY GRAINS

Tylor Noel hands out samples of Country Grains bread.

Since 1996, Kelly and Albert Hewitt have been baking breads and other items, such as cookies and muffins, with only natural ingredients like whole wheat flour and honey. Their bread does not contain preservatives or fillers and is baked at their Sylvania store on Sylvania Avenue. Customers can select from white or wheat, Challah, loaves baked with onions and garlic or cheese or breads sweetened with strawberries, blueberries, cranberries, apricots or raisins. On a typical night, they will produce over fifteen hundred loaves. Their bread is popular in the Toledo area and is carried at several local stores, like Walt Churchill's Markets, Sautter's Markets and at area farmers' markets.

CURB'S CANDLE CO.

J.P. Rady and Julie Jordan have been selling their candles for thirteen years and used to sell at the Erie Street Market when it was in operation next to the Toledo Farmers' Market. They enjoy coming to the Toledo Farmers' Market because it is "a friendly, happy work environment." J.P. remembers coming to the market as a young boy, since his grandfather used to grow and sell garlic. J.P.'s father can remember coming down to the market in the late 1940s. He and his older brother sat on top of the crates full of garlic, swaying back and forth as the loaded truck made its way to the market.

Egg & Honey

www.eggandhoney.com

Amelia Contreras has been baking her sourdough breads for three years and regularly sells out by midday at Saturday's market. Her breads are made from scratch using sourdough starter. To give her breads their deep flavor, Amelia uses the best ingredients—like maple syrup and honey and fruits from local sources—whenever possible. Amelia explains that she came up with the name Egg & Honey because "eggs and honey are two of the oldest and simplest of human foods. They represent the goal of respecting traditions and the past as keys to eating for the future."

Flying Rhino Coffee and Chocolates

www.flyingrhinocoffee.com

Ralph and Gini Behrendt have always loved coffee. Both former glass artists, they had the opportunity to try many different coffees as they traveled to art shows across the country. Gini remembered sitting at a coffee shop on a trip and wondering, "How come I cannot get my coffee at home to taste like this?" Thus began their quest for the perfect cup of coffee. One of Gini's students showed them how she roasted her own coffee beans at home, and soon Ralph took up roasting their own beans—a half pound of coffee at a time—in a small roaster.

Ralph also took up chocolate making and was dubbed the "Midnight Chocolatier" by friends and family. "I would make art glass by day, roast coffee in the afternoon and make chocolate at night," Ralph cheerfully explained.

When the Behrendts were caught up in the prospect of a career change, coffee seemed to fit them perfectly. They found a large vintage coffee bean roaster on eBay and drove to Wisconsin to bring their find home. The Royal #5 roaster they procured on eBay launched their new enterprise: Flying Rhino Coffee and Chocolates. Since October 2005, the Behrendts have been serving coffee to shoppers at the Toledo Farmers' Market.

FRUTH'S SUGARHOUSE GREENHOUSE & FERAL

Ilene Fruth has been selling at the Toledo Farmers' Market for over fifteen years and has been growing plants for almost two decades. Fruth's Sugarhouse Greenhouse & Floral features annual bedding and vegetable plants, perennials and herbs. The Fruths have also been making maple syrup since 1977.

GARDEN NURSERY

www.raisingrarities.com

Roger Zielinski remembers visiting the market at a young age with his father. With vivid memories of the gravel roads, the hucksters and the caged chickens, Roger recalls busy days at the market. Now, Roger sells plants and organic produce there. Roger is the founder and creator of the Garden Sanctuary at Common Space Too, which is a Center for Creativity and the Arts operated by the Arts Council Lake Erie West. Started in 1994, the Garden Sanctuary is a display of antique roses and seventeenth-century gardens. Roger has a passion for lady's slipper orchids and rare plants hardy enough to survive the winters of Northwest Ohio. Roger runs the Garden Nursery on Holland Sylvania Road and is sought out by homeowners and businesses that rely on his talent for designing with natural floral elements. In addition, Zielinski runs his online site, where he sells lady's slippers throughout the country.

GERTIE'S BBQ SAUCE

www.gertiesbbqsauce.com

Gertie's Premium Barbeque Sauce was named after Kyle Baker's mother, Gertrude. The BBQ sauce is perfect as a grilling sauce but can also be used as a meatloaf glaze, salad dressing or dipping sauce.

Goodfellows Farm

Janice Carpenter and her family, which includes her children and several grandchildren, sell at the Toledo Farmers' Market on Saturdays. Janice enjoys the tradition of selling at the market and is pleased to see her grandchildren learn skills that will help them in life—being nice to customers and sharpening math skills by making change. The Goodfellows Farm is located in Ida, Michigan, where the Carpenters all help plow, plant and harvest some of what they provide at the market. Everyone helps on the farm, even the grandchildren. They have been selling at the market for approximately twenty-five years.

Great Lakes Bullfrog BBQ, LLC

Diana and David DeBacker have been making sauce for fifteen years and started selling at the Toledo Farmers' Market in August 2010. Their Great Lakes Bullfrog BBQ sauce comes in two flavors: original, made with rum, and spicy apple, made with apple cider. They also make a seasoning salt and a BBQ meat rub. The Great Lakes Bullfrog BBQ name was inspired by Toledo's nickname: Frogtown. Toledo received the nickname due to its proximity to what was once the Great Black Swamp.

Heaven's Gate Soy Candles

www.heavensgatesoy.com

Shoppers keep coming back to purchase Heaven's Gate Soy Candles for themselves and as gifts. Everyone has a different favorite, from original to seasonal scents, like Drunkin' Mosquito, which contains citronella, margarita and lime to help keep mosquitoes away. Jacquie and Tom Olender create their candles from soy wax from midwestern soybeans and hand pour each into containers from Toledo's Libbey Glass. The soybean wax, cotton cored wicks and the finest fragrances give their candles unique appeal. Soy burns slower, cooler, cleaner and twice as long as paraffin wax. At their shop in downtown Sylvania, the Olenders carry not only their candles but also a supply of products from other local businesses.

HOMESTEAD SOAPS LLC

www.fromthehomestead.com

Lori Diver began making her own soap after her daughter was diagnosed with eczema. She struggled to find a gentle soap or body wash free of synthetic chemicals and petroleum derivatives. Eventually, Lori started making her own soap and noticed that not only did her daughter's skin improve, but also the skin of her whole family improved.

Lori makes her soaps with a blend of rich plant oils that condition and soothe the skin. Essential oils, organic herbs and other botanicals are added depending on the recipe of each natural bar. Lori has a strong commitment to keeping her soap environmentally friendly. She contributes part of her profits to organizations such as Polar Bears International and the Orangutan Foundation.

JEFFERS

Max Jeffers, who comes from a long line of farmers, takes pride in what he grows. "My father was always particular about quality," Max said. In Cleveland, Max is known as the Zucchini Man.[59] For at least thirty-five years, Max hauled zucchini to the Cleveland Produce Terminal, where it was sold to grocery stores throughout the region. They were usually snatched up by produce buyer Peter Ross, who supplied approximately fifteen Cleveland-based Heinen's, Inc. stores.[60] Max continued to deliver his zucchini to Cleveland until 2010. Max and his family continue to tend plants at their Grand Rapids farm and sell what they grow at the greenhouse and local markets, including the Toledo Farmers' Market.

Ernest Jeffers stands with a loaded truck. "He was always particular about quality," Max Jeffers said about his father. *Courtesy of Judy Peper.*

Max's brother Charlie continued to run the produce stand and orchards on Route 24. Their father purchased the farm in 1936 and continued to expand year after year. Jeffers Gardens was known for its melons, squash, peaches, potatoes, apples and more. *Courtesy of Judy Peper.*

JENTZEN FARMS

Brian Jentzen is a third-generation farmer well known for having fresh and dried herbs at the Toledo Farmers' Market. Brian started selling at the Toledo Farmers' Market approximately seven years ago. In addition, Jentzen Farms also sells at the Detroit, Dundee and Monroe Farmers' Markets in Michigan and at the Perrysburg Farmers' Market in Ohio. Jentzen Farms provides produce of all kinds and practices sustainable agriculture using cover crops, natural fertilizer and natural pest control.

The Jentzen family in 2004. *Courtesy of Brian Jentzen.*

Karen Freytag, at the kettle, and her son, Chris, prepare kettle corn for a festival in 2000. *Courtesy of Karen Freytag.*

KAREN ANNE'S KETTLE KORN

This year marks the twelfth year that Karen and Max Freytag have been selling their kettle corn at the Toledo Farmers' Market. They also sell at the Perrysburg Farmers' Market, at Westgate Farmers' Market in West Toledo and at several fairs and festivals throughout the year.

KONSTANTINOS

Konstantinos Konstandas has been selling at the Toledo Farmers' Market since the early 1990s. Konstantinos was originally from Greece, where he grew wheat and tended olive groves. Now, he sells plants and grows vegetables to take to the market. Even though he admits that each year gets harder, he continues to do all of his own weeding, often by hand, and ties each and every tomato plant to supports as it grows tall.

Konstantinos Konstandas continues to do all of his own weeding, often by hand, and ties each and every tomato plant to supports as it grows tall.

Local Liberty Market

libertylocalmarket.com

Elizabeth Fallon sells her own specialty jams, infused vinegars and Meadow Maid cheeses at the Toledo Farmers' Market. With a degree in nutrition, her goal is to raise awareness of how making healthy food choices can have a positive impact on lives and communities. Elizabeth gets her inspiration for her herbed vinegars from her mother, who is a natural at making herbed vinegars with herbs from her garden. Elizabeth especially enjoys making berry jams because of their wonderful flavors and colors.

Meadow Maid cheese is made from milk from healthy, grass-fed cows near Fredericktown, Ohio. Meadow Maid cheese is distributed to farmers' markets throughout Ohio, and Elizabeth Fallon is pleased to offer a variety of cheeses.

LOUIS KEIL & SONS

The Louis Keil & Sons farm was started in 1954 by Louis E. Keil Sr. and his sons, Louis Jr. and Walter. Located on Central Avenue, Louis Keil & Sons grow annuals, perennials, vegetable starts, hanging baskets, herbs and seasonal produce. Even though the business is now managed by four of Keil Sr.'s grandsons—Norm, Anthony, Michael and Tim—the whole family can be found helping with different areas of the business.

Evelyn Keil is known for her herbs that she harvests by hand. At home, she prepares produce for the winter months, canning and freezing all that she can. She cooks and bakes everything from scratch. "She has never written her recipes down; they are all in her head. It's a dash of this and a dash of that," her granddaughter Becky Keil Kornmeier said. When asked about his mother, Norm Keil smiled and replied, "She keeps all us Keils in line."

LUMBREZER

Tom and Margie Lumbrezer are best known for their tomatoes, yellow sweet corn and Candy onions. Tom grew up on a farm, and at the age of sixteen, he started going to the Toledo Farmers' Market with his brother to sell their plants and produce. Margie has been coming to the market with Tom since they were married. The two of them manage their two-and-a-half-acre farm in Swanton, Ohio, doing all of the work themselves.

Tom and Margie Lumbrezer are known for their tomatoes, yellow sweet corn and Candy onions, which they grow on their two-and-a-half-acre farm. One summer, they grew thirty-five thousand candy onions. *Courtesy of Tom and Margie Lumbrezer.*

Main Creek Farms

Main Creek Farms is located in Weston, Ohio, and is run by Josh Main, a fourth-generation farmer. Josh comes from a long line of farmers on both sides of his family. His great-grandparents Elmer and Loretta Puehler were vendors at the Toledo Farmers' Market, and his parents and their families continued farming through the years.

Josh is currently attending Bowling Green State University and majoring in accounting and supply chain management. As an extension of his FFA (Future Farmers of America) project, Josh had the idea to sell canned beef and frozen cuts of beef at the market. At the age of fourteen, he approached his parents with the idea and has been selling at the market ever since.

Main Creek Farms is known for its high-quality beef. The family has been raising cows since 1906, and they raise their animals without hormones, steroids or unnatural products. In addition to their frozen retail cuts, they sell canned beef that is fully cooked for a fast dinner. Canned beef can be used in soups, stews, tacos, beef and noodles, enchiladas, barbecue sandwiches, burritos and more.

Elmer and Loretta Puehler's son Howard stands with a pig on their farm in Swanton, Ohio. *Courtesy of Main Creek Farms.*

Josh Main still practices traditions and standards put in place by his grandfather Elmer, and he only sells products that he would feed to his own family.

Main Creek Farms is a family business, and Josh's aunt Hazel Schaller sells at the neighboring stall. Hazel carries handcrafted items and homegrown popcorn.

OSBORN FARMS

The history of the Osborn family at the Toledo Farmers' Market goes back approximately eighty years to when Henry Osborn Sr. starting selling there. Now the fourth generation—Shawn and his wife, Dianne, and Shawn's brothers, Mike and Matt—have taken over the operations of the farm. They grow and sell a wide variety of fruits and vegetables and are best known for their green and yellow beans. The three brothers keep a photograph of their father, Larry, up in their stall. Larry is well remembered by customers as being a wonderful and friendly man.

Parran's Greenhouse and Farm

Brandon Parran has been coming to the Toledo Farmers' Market since he was sixteen. The original greenhouse and farm expanded into two and a half acres of greenhouses and approximately sixty acres of produce in Ida, Michigan. The farm was started by Brandon's father, Mike. "He started with bare land and a pickup truck," Brandon explained. The Parran family sells at their two stores—in Ida and Monroe, Michigan—and at several markets. They also offer pick-your-own strawberries and tomatoes.

Sage Organics

www.sageorganicsohio.com

Elizabeth Bergman and her brother, Henry, started Sage Organics to meet the demand for organic produce. Her farm, located in Genoa, Ohio, continues to grow as she adds more items each year. In three years, she has expanded to two acres and two hoop houses—simple, unheated greenhouse-like structures covered in heavy greenhouse plastic. Liz grows over thirty vegetables and herbs and is known for her gourmet salad mixes, cooking greens, heirloom tomatoes and garlic. She has put her culinary background to good use around the farm and offers cooking tips and recipes to customers. Liz also raises chickens—both broilers and laying hens—pastured pigs and honeybees.

Schmittuz Gardens

George Dabrunz, along with his sons Tim and Scott, operates Schmittuz Gardens on Port Clinton Road in Fremont, Ohio. The business began in 1913, when George's uncle, George Schmittuz, delivered produce to over forty grocery stores in Fremont. Large grocery stores and chain stores moved into Fremont, and the smaller stores slowly folded. The large grocery stores ordered produce from their distributors in other states, so local produce sales to grocery stores dwindled. The family has been coming to sell their produce at the Toledo Farmers' Market since 1966. The Dabrunzes also sell at Jamie's Flea Market in Lorain County, Ohio, and the Detroit Eastern Market in Michigan.

Tim, George and Scott Dabrunz stand in front of the 1938 model truck their uncle, George Schmittuz, bought for his produce and flower deliveries. Schmittuz bought the truck in Detroit, Michigan, for $900 and continued to drive it until he was ninety years old. *Photograph by Jodi Ashoftehfard.*

Scott Dabrunz sits atop Sally, his family's horse, in 1952. The family used horses on the farm until 1956. *Courtesy of George Dabrunz.*

George Schmittuz built his first greenhouse in 1918, when his wife, Lily, wanted to join the local garden club. Eventually, he started raising plants for sale and built additional greenhouses. The Dabrunzes still use the original greenhouses and cold frames built by their uncle. The cold frames are raised flower beds that have removable glass tops and allow the Dabrunzes to start many spring plants several weeks earlier than the growing season.

Scott and Tim Dabrunz started helping at the market when they were teenagers. They remember driving into Toledo the night before market day and stocking up on soda pop and candy for the night. They placed their sleeping bags on the benches and tried to get as much sleep as they could before the market started in the morning.

Scrumptious

Shannon Marruquin has always shopped at the Toledo Farmers' Market for her flowers and vegetables. For the last three years, she has been a regular vendor, selling her scrumptious baked goods. Considering her display of desserts, it is hard to believe that Shannon originally had no interest in learning how to bake. But after she married into a large family, she was expected to bring a dessert to every family function. After honing her baking skills, she began baking for others and eventually became a vendor at the market.

Se~Em~Da Farms & Gardens

Se-Em-Da Farms & Gardens was started by three friends: Sean Wonder, Emily Prasuhn and Daniel Stacy. Located in Green Springs, Ohio, they offer beef, chicken, pork, eggs and produce grown on their farm for sale at the Toledo Farmers' Market.

Sugar Cube, LLC

Armed with a culinary arts degree and a lifetime of practice, Vivian Miller used to make wedding cakes and has sold her stunning baked goods at the Toledo Farmers' Market for the last four years. Leslie Jackson, Vivian's daughter, often helps with preparing the baked goods and selling on

Saturday. Leslie grew up with good food, and they make it a priority to make baked goods that have simple and fresh ingredients—ingredients that can be readily identified and easily pronounced.

T & J Cottage Gourmet

Tammy Saunders offers spices, dip mixes and flavored sea salts to the market. Though relatively new to the market as a vendor, she has been coming to shop for years. "Even though I have only been selling for a short time, I feel very much at home at the market," she remarked. "The vendors are like a big family, and they were all very kind and welcoming when I first started."

Thomas Family Farm

The Thomas family is one of the first African American farmers to sell at the Toledo Farmers' Market. When they started selling in 1947, their stall was located at the end of the market. Even though it was not the most visible spot, the Thomases supplied turnip greens, black-eyed peas, poke salad and Kentucky Wonder pole beans and were soon sought out by shoppers for their southern favorites. Henry and Katie Thomas came to Toledo from Yazoo City, Mississippi, after Henry served in the navy during World War II. Katie still lives on the family farm on Eber Road in Holland that the family has farmed for decades.

Katie Thomas and her daughter, Ella Mae Hall, were Toledo Farmers' Market vendors who participated in Market Day at Promenade Park. The market was set up at the park temporarily on August 21, 1986, to help boost awareness of the downtown market. *Courtesy of Eleanor Billau.*

Floyd, Ed and Lynne Weiland at the Toledo Farmers' Market in 2001. *Courtesy of Eleanor Billau.*

Ed and Lynne Weiland

For the last forty years, Ed and Lynne Weiland have been selling at the Toledo Farmers' Market. For many years, Lynne's father, Harold Hassen, helped at the market. Ed's brother Floyd also helped, until his death in May 2011. The Weilands raise asparagus, sweet corn, green onions, peppers, broccoli, cauliflower, green beans, butternut and acorn squash and pumpkins. Ed and Lynne have enjoyed their years at the market. "If and when we retire, we will miss all our dear customers," Lynne said.

Wenz Greenhouse

Wenz Greenhouse is located on the same land that has been in the Wenz family for six generations. The greenhouse business that now spans over six acres started when Oscar Wenz built the first greenhouse in 1930. The business now supplies bedding plants, vegetable starts, hanging baskets and more. Oscar's son Don can remember coming to the Toledo Farmers' Market when he was about eight years old, when it was located indoors at the Erie Street location, only a few feet from the present-day market stalls. Stalls were identified with metal signs, and his family had stall number forty-nine. In the days before plastic flats and trays,

Don and Dolores Wenz and their daughter, Kathy, work for the family business that Oscar Wenz started in 1930.

Don's family made them all with wood. Don and his wife, Dolores, have two children—Kathy and Jeff—and both still help their parents with the business.

WILLY'S FAMOUS SALSA

www.willyssalsa.com

Inspired by a recipe shared from a friend in Mexico, Willy's Famous Salsa is now a favorite for many shoppers of the Toledo Farmers' Market. Dennis Dickey used the recipe to make salsa for his friends and family and served it to customers while running a Nevada restaurant in 1985. With urging from friends and family, Dennis finally decided to produce Willy's Famous Salsa for everyone to enjoy. Available in seven different flavors, Willy's Famous Salsa is produced in Bowling Green, Ohio, and can be found in the refrigerated sections at local grocery stores and markets. Additionally, several flavors have found their way into markets in Michigan, Indiana, Illinois, Kentucky and West Virginia.

Wines Bee Yard

www.winesbeeyard.com

Beekeepers Debbie and Jim Wines live just north of Toledo, in Palmyra, Michigan. They manage five separate apiaries, or bee yards, and do not use chemicals or medications to treat their bees. The Wines sell their products at some local stores and several area markets, including the Toledo Farmers' Market. Besides selling honey, they also sell honey mustard, whipped honey spreads, bee pollen, lip balm and candles made from beeswax.

Debbie Wines, wearing her queen bee hat, stands ready to talk about the importance of local honey in 2009. *Courtesy of Debbie Wines.*

Jim Wines shows a frame from the inside of a hive to his young apprentice, Lily Diver, daughter of Lori Diver, in 2010. *Courtesy of Debbie Wines.*

WITT'S ORCHARD & CIDER MILL

Witt's Orchard in Oak Harbor, Ohio, has been in business for over forty years, tending to over fifteen thousand trees. They have an amazing variety: seventy kinds of apples, over twenty kinds of peaches, twenty varieties of plums, ten kinds of pears, six varieties of Asian pears and six kinds of nectarines.

OTHER VENDORS

Other vendors for the 2011 season include Blueberry Hill Orchard, Bob's Best Salsa, Bortilotti Gourmet, Creque Farms, Earth Grrrl, Dentel Farms, Farnsel Farms, Goscik Farms, Hecklinger's Greenhouse, Holtz Farms, Jewelry by Dana, Monteleone Foods, Nick's World Famous Hotdogs, North Branch Nursery, Ohio Farm Direct, The Perfect Arrangement, Randy Thurman, Rhodes Garden Fresh, Rhues Farms, Selby Thames, Tucker Farms, Vittore Farms and Zemnicki Farms.

Recipes

The belly rules the mind.
—Spanish proverb

Kitchen Equivalency Chart

Pinch	1/8 teaspoon or less
3 teaspoons	1 tablespoon
2 tablespoons	1/8 cup
4 tablespoons	1/4 cup
16 tablespoons.	1 cup
5 tablespoons + 1 teaspoon	1/3 cup
4 ounces	1/2 cup
8 ounces	1 cup
16 ounces	1 pound
1 ounce	2 tablespoons fat or liquid
1 cup of liquid	1/2 pint
2 cups of liquid	1 pint
4 cups of liquid	1 quart
2 pints	1 quart
1 quart	4 cups
4 quarts	1 gallon
8 quarts	1 peck (such as apples, pears, etc.)

FOOD EQUIVALENCY CHART

1 pound flour	4 cups
1 pound cornmeal	3 cups
1 medium lemon	3 tablespoons juice
1 medium apple	1 cup
3–4 medium oranges	1 cup juice
1 medium onion	½ cup
1 pound unshelled walnuts	1½ to 1¾ cups
1 pound sugar	2 cups
1 pound powdered sugar	3½ cups
1 pound brown sugar	2½ cups
7 ounces spaghetti	4 cups cooked
1½–2 cups noodles (uncooked)	2–3 cups cooked
1¼ cups macaroni (uncooked)	2¼ cooked
1 cup long-grain rice (uncooked)	3–4 cups cooked
28 saltine crackers	1 cup fine crumbs
¼ pound butter	½ cup
1 pound cocoa	4 cups
14 squares graham crackers	1 cup fine crumbs
22 vanilla wafers	1 cup fine crumbs
1½ slices bread	1 cup soft crumbs
1 slice bread	¼ cup fine, dry crumbs
8–10 egg whites	1 cup
10–12 egg yolks	1 cup
4–5 whole eggs	1 cup
¼ pound nuts (chopped)	1 cup
1 pound almonds	3½ cups
1 pound raisins	3½ cups
1 pound rice	2⅓ cups
1 banana (mashed)	⅓ cup
1 pound coffee	5 cups
1 pound ground meat or hamburger	2 cups

Berry Equivalents

These equivalents are approximate and vary due to berry size.

1 pint of berries..2½ cups whole berries
1 pint of berries..2½ cups sliced berries
1 pint of berries..1¾ cups pureed berries
1 ½–2 quarts are needed for a 9-inch pie

Squash Equivalents

These equivalents are approximate and vary due to squash size.

1 pound peeled squash...............................1 cup cooked, mashed
2½ pound whole squash ....2¾–3 cups pureed
1 pound trimmed squash ....2 cups cooked pieces
1 medium-size (approximately 15 to 20 pounds) pumpkin will yield 5 to 7 quarts of cooked pumpkin.

Substitutions

When used for cooking and baking, these substitutions can be made in recipes.

1 cup whipping cream	⅓ cup butter plus ¾ cup milk
1 package dry yeast	2 teaspoons dry yeast
½ cup honey	⅝ cup sugar with ⅛ cup water
½ cup molasses	½ cup honey
½ cup buttermilk	½ cup milk plus 1½ teaspoons vinegar
½ cup sour milk	½ cup milk plus 1½ teaspoons lemon juice
½ cup sour cream	½ cup plain unflavored yogurt
1 teaspoon baking powder	½ tsp. cream of tartar with ¼ teaspoon baking soda
1 tablespoon flour (for thickening)	2 egg yolks or ½ tablespoon cornstarch

1 cup tomato juice	½ cup tomato sauce plus ½ cup water
1 large marshmallow	10 miniature marshmallows
1 cup ketchup or chili sauce	1 cup tomato sauce plus ½ cup sugar and 2 tablespoons vinegar
1 square unsweetened chocolate	3 tablespoons cocoa with 1 tablespoon butter

BAKING DISH SUBSTITUTIONS

8-inch square (6–8 cups)	1½ quarts
11x7x2-inch or 8-inch square (8 cups)	2 quarts
9-inch square (10 cups)	2½ quarts
13x9x2-inch (12–14 cups)	3 quarts

A NOTE ABOUT INGREDIENTS

BUTTER: In most cases, salted and unsalted butter are used interchangeably with the recipes in this book. Shortening is made from hydrogenated vegetable oils and has virtually no flavor. Margarine is also made from vegetable oils that are refined and processed, while butter is a natural dairy product. Neither shortening nor margarine is used in any of the recipes in this book. Some people, especially those with dairy allergies, have luck with substituting butter with coconut oil and sustainable palm oil or other natural fats.

CREAM, WHIPPED CREAM: Use real whipping cream and avoid processed toppings. Be aware that some larger dairy manufacturers will add carrageenan to their whipped cream in order to make it thick. Read labels carefully.

SALT: In all recipes where called for, natural sea salt is used. Natural sea salt is a unique color because of the natural trace minerals it contains. Avoid salts that have been bleached and contain anti-caking agents.

SUCANAT: Sucanat is sugar extracted from sugar cane. Brown sugar or turbinado sugar can be used in place of sucanat. In some cases, people use all of these interchangeably in recipes without a discernable difference in the final product.

Vanilla: Use real vanilla extract in baking and avoid the cheaper synthetic imitation vanilla. Real vanilla is made from the pods, while the flavor in imitation vanilla is chemically created.

A Note about Methods

Blanching: When freezing some vegetables, blanching is required. Blanching is a process of quickly cooking in boiling water. This helps kill any bacteria and slows vitamin and mineral loss. Most vegetables that require blanching only need to be in the boiling water for one to two minutes.

Creaming: In recipes that call for creaming the butter and sugar, take 2 to 3 minutes to do so. Taking the time to properly cream the butter and sugar can make a difference in the texture of baked goods.

Flash Freezing: Flash freezing is freezing items separately on trays before packaging them together. This prevents the food items from lumping together in the freezer container.

Folding: Sometimes recipes call for folding whipped eggs or fruit into batter. To fold, gently turn the whipped eggs or fruit into the batter with a spatula just enough to combine.

Peaks: When blending whipping cream or eggs, the recipe may call to do so until peaks form. This means to mix until the mixture gets frothy. When the blender is pulled away from the mixture, it will leave a small mound or peak. A stiff peak will stand up straight while a soft peak will flop over.

Steaming: Inexpensive steam racks or baskets come in different sizes and can be placed in a saucepan. Place the steam rack over 1 to 2 inches of water and bring water to a boil. Place cut vegetables into steam rack and cover. Most vegetables only need to steam for about 2 minutes. Frozen vegetables and thicker pieces will take longer. Potatoes can take 15 to 30 minutes, depending on the size of the pieces.

Washing: Washing produce reduces the storage life. If produce has not been washed it can be stored longer and washed right before preparing and serving.

HERBS

Jentzen Farms in Monroe, Michigan, is known for its fine herbs. This list of herbs and their uses was adapted from the list the Jentzen family provides to their customers.

Cinnamon basil has a distinct cinnamon taste and odor. Cinnamon basil is especially great in tomato dishes, pasta sauces and soups. Some gardeners use cinnamon basil as a companion plant to repel aphids, mites and tomato hornworms.

Lemon basil is intensely fragrant of lemon. It is ideal for teas, ice cream and homemade potpourris.

Opal basil is an excellent seasoning for basil vinegar and turns the vinegar a beautiful red color.

Sweet basil is a basic for all tomato dishes, marinara or spaghetti sauces, soups and stews. Sweet basil is also great in meatloaf, shellfish, vegetable dishes, omelets, salads, cheese dishes, pasta and pesto.

Catnip can be used to make a wonderfully soothing tea. Dried catnip can also be used in homemade cat toys.

Chives are a member of the onion family, but they are quite mild and go well in many dishes. Snip the green leaves of chives into eggs, sauces, soups and salads. The purple blossoms can be used as a garnish or to make delicious chive blossom vinegar.

Garlic chives have a garlic-infused flavor. Snip the green leaves of garlic chives and use in salads or stir-fries.

Cilantro is usually used in Mexican salsa, Indian cuisine, chutney, rice dishes, stews, sausage and fowl dishes. The seed of the cilantro plant is known as coriander.

Dill is used for dilly bread, shellfish, fish, cabbage, carrots, potato salad, coleslaw, cucumber salads, green beans and dill pickles. Dill is also great in soups, eggs and cheese dishes.

Lavender has a clean scent that is used in potpourris, sachets used to scent linen drawers and soap. Lavender also looks lovely in dried flower arrangements.

Lemon balm adds an interesting flavor to salads, soups and stews. A tea made from the dried leaves is a favorite of the Jentzen family.

Lovage can be used like celery in soups, stews, salads, sauces and casseroles.

Sweet marjoram leaves add a strong, spicy flavor to soups, sauces, stuffing, stews, sausage and meatloaf.

Apple mint has a sweet taste with a cool aftertaste. It is great for tea, ice cream and mojitos. Apple mint can also be used for apple mint jelly.

Lemon mint can be used in fruit salads, fruit punch, tea and ice cream.

Lime mint can be used in fruit salads, tea and fruit punch. Lime mint also makes a nice addition to homemade potpourris.

Orange mint can be used like all other mints.

Peppermint goes great with fruit, lemonade, ice cream, split pea soup and potatoes. Peppermint can also be used to make a mint jelly that can be used on lamb.

Spearmint goes well with carrots, peas and potatoes. Spearmint is also great for making a mint sauce for roasted lamb.

Greek oregano is used in Italian, Spanish and Mexican cooking. It has a hot, spicy flavor that complements almost all tomato dishes, beef and lamb stew, gravies, soups, salads, pizzas and casseroles. Oregano is also great with potatoes and artichokes.

Parsley (curly or Italian) can be added to almost any savory dish, especially fish, poultry and vegetables, to help bring out the flavors of other spices.

Rosemary is appealing in dumplings, sauces, biscuits and preserves. It goes well with chicken, in meatloaf and with lamb and pork. Rosemary is also great with mushrooms, potatoes, peas and lima beans.

Sage is often used in sausages, omelets, cheese dishes, stews and bean dishes. Sage works well flavoring rich meats like pork and duck and is a popular companion with onion for poultry stuffing.

Thyme is indispensible in French cooking. Thyme is great for seasoning rich meats and fish. Thyme is also wonderful with mushrooms, tomatoes and peas and in sauces, soups and salads.

Lemon Thyme has a delightful lemon flavor that goes well with fish and chicken and in salads and tea.

Jentzen Farms in Monroe, Michigan, is known for its fine herbs. Whenever possible, it still uses horses on the farm instead of modern machinery. *Courtesy of Brian Jentzen.*

APPLE TIPS

Keep apples crisp longer by storing them in the refrigerator.
Grated apples can be added to just about any muffin and cake recipe.

Apple Butter Frosting

This apple butter frosting is a thin frosting, great for spreading on cupcakes and muffins.

4 tablespoons butter, softened
1¾ cups powdered sugar
¼ cup apple butter
2 tablespoons sour cream
¼ teaspoon almond extract

With hand mixer, cream butter and sugar until light and fluffy. Add apple butter, sour cream and almond extract. Beat until light and fluffy.

Apple Cake

This recipe for Apple Cake was submitted by Betty Jeffers. It is a family favorite that she makes every year. This cake is perfect topped with cream cheese frosting.

2 cups all-purpose flour
2 teaspoons baking soda
2 cups sugar
2 teaspoons cinnamon
Dash salt
4 eggs
1 cup butter
4 cups peeled apple chunks
2 cups chopped nuts

Mix flour, baking soda, sugar, cinnamon and salt together in a large bowl. Blend in eggs and butter by hand. Add apples and nuts and stir until thoroughly combined. Pour batter into a greased 9x13 pan. Bake for 60 minutes at 300 degrees. Remove, let cool and frost.

APPLE CHUTNEY

This tasty apple chutney is perfect served alongside pork chops or baked ham.

4 tablespoons butter
2 cups tart apples (chopped)
3 tablespoons Sucanat
2 tablespoons golden raisins
2 tablespoons dried cranberries
½ teaspoon cinnamon
¼ teaspoon nutmeg
1 teaspoon lemon juice
⅓ cup apple cider or juice

Heat butter in saucepan. Add all ingredients and cook over medium heat until apple pieces are tender and cider has boiled away. If needed, add a bit more apple cider or juice to keep the mixture from scorching. Makes about 2 cups. Serve warm or chilled.

APPLE CREAM PENNIES

This recipe will create about 65 to 70 1-inch cookies.

2½ cups all-purpose flour
½ teaspoon baking soda
¼ teaspoon salt
1½ cups Sucanat
1 cup butter, softened
2 eggs
2 teaspoons vanilla extract

<u>Filling</u>
8 ounces cream cheese, softened
¼ cup sugar
¼ cup apple butter

In a medium bowl, mix flour, baking soda and salt. In a separate bowl, blend Sucanat and butter with an electric mixer using medium speed. Add eggs and vanilla and beat until light and fluffy. Add flour mixture and blend at low speed until just combined. Do not overmix. Shape dough into small, approximately half-inch balls and place on an ungreased cookie sheet about 1 inch apart. Bake for 10 minutes at 300 degrees. Do not let cookies brown. Transfer cookies to a cool, flat surface.

Filling
Blend cream cheese and sugar on medium speed until fluffy. Add apple butter and beat until smooth. Just before serving, spread 1 teaspoon of filling onto the flat side of a cookie and top with another cookie to create a sandwich. Repeat until all cookies are assembled.

Apple Crumble

Topping
¾ cup wheat flour
½ cup Sucanat (or brown sugar)
½ teaspoon ground cinnamon
5 tablespoons butter, melted

Filling
4 apples, peeled and sliced
½ cup sugar
2 tablespoons flour
½ teaspoon ground cinnamon

Heat oven to 350 degrees. To make topping, combine flour, sucanat and cinnamon in a small bowl. Add butter and mix until thoroughly combined. Topping will be crumbly. Set mixture aside.

Filling
Combine sliced apples with sugar, flour and cinnamon. Stir well and pour into a 9-inch baking dish. Crumble the topping over the fruit mixture. Bake for 40 minutes or until apple mixture begins to bubble. Serve warm.

Apple Enchiladas

1 large apple
2 tablespoons Sucanat
½ teaspoon cinnamon
4 fajita-sized tortillas

Topping
2 tablespoons butter
2 teaspoons sugar

Peel and slice or chop large apple into small pieces. Place apple pieces in a small bowl with Sucanat and cinnamon. Make sure the apple pieces are thoroughly coated and spread mixture evenly between the 4 tortillas. Make sure filling stays down the center of the tortilla, leaving a small space at each end of tortilla. Slightly fold in the edges. Then bring one side of the tortilla over the filling, and then the other, wrapping the filling completely in the tortilla. Repeat with each tortilla. Lay each side by side, seam-side down, in an 8-inch square baking dish. Melt the butter for the topping and mix in the sugar. Pour topping over the apple enchiladas and let stand for 30 minutes. Meanwhile, preheat oven to 350 degrees. Bake for 20 minutes. Makes 4 servings.

Applesauce

It is best to ask the apple experts at the market which apples are best to use for applesauce. However, experimenting with different types can be fun.

9 apples, peeled and cored
1½ cups water
⅓ cup sugar, or to taste
1 tablespoon cinnamon, or to taste

Boil apples until tender, approximately 20 minutes. Run apples through a food mill for fine applesauce or simply mash with a potato masher for a chunky applesauce. Add sugar and cinnamon to taste.

Arugula Pesto

Recipe submitted by Sage Organics.

4 cups packed fresh arugula
1 tablespoon minced garlic
Salt
Freshly ground pepper
1 cup pure olive oil
2 tablespoons toasted pine nuts, plus 1 tablespoon set aside
½ cup freshly grated parmesan

Roughly chop the arugula and put in a blender. Add garlic, salt and ground pepper to taste, olive oil and 2 tablespoons of pine nuts. Blend for at least 30 seconds. The green of the arugula will thoroughly color the oil. Add parmesan cheese and pulse to combine. The pesto will keep for several days in a tightly sealed container in the refrigerator. Take pesto out of the refrigerator so it comes to room temperature before serving. Add additional 1 tablespoon of toasted pine nuts if desired.

Preparing Asparagus

Asparagus can be rinsed by being held upside down and gently swishing the ends in cold water. The tough, woody bottoms can be snapped off.

Roasted Asparagus

1 pound asparagus spears
2 tablespoons extra virgin olive oil
2 garlic cloves, minced
Salt

Preheat oven to 400 degrees. Wash asparagus and snap off woody ends. Place spears in a single layer in a shallow pan. Mix olive oil and garlic together and coat asparagus with the mixture. Lightly sprinkle spears with salt. Bake for 10 to 20 minutes, as preferred. (The longer it is baked, the crispier the ends will be.)

Chocolate Avocado Loaf

1½ cups all-purpose flour
1 teaspoon baking powder
3 tablespoons unsweetened cocoa powder
¼ teaspoon salt
⅓ cup avocado, mashed
1 cup milk
¼ cup olive oil
1 teaspoon vanilla extract
1 cup sugar

Preheat oven to 350 degrees. In a bowl, mix together flour, baking powder, cocoa powder and salt. In a large bowl, mix together the avocado, milk, olive oil and vanilla extract. Add sugar and mix until blended. Slowly add flour mixture and keep stirring until well blended. Pour batter into greased loaf pan. Bake for 30 to 35 minutes, or until a knife inserted in the center comes out clean. Let cool. Slice and serve.

Other Uses for Barbecue Sauce

Barbecue sauce can be used in countless ways. It can be used on burgers, Sloppy Joes and meatloaf; used as a dip for sweet potato fries or chicken nuggets; and added to baked beans to give them a spicy taste.

Sweet Basil Dip

1 cup plain yogurt
1 cup fresh basil leaves, finely chopped
¼ teaspoon salt
Ground black pepper to taste

Mix ingredients well and serve. Makes about 1½ cups.

Beans

Beans are relatively easy to use in dishes without having to resort to canned varieties, and they are easy to store dry in containers until needed.

Beans should be soaked overnight. Combine one cup of dried beans with three cups water and place covered in the refrigerator. Drain the beans and rinse well under running water. To cook, bring three cups of water per one cup beans to a full boil. Reduce heat and simmer until tender. Or place beans in a slow cooker. Combine three cups of water per one cup beans and cook on low until tender.

One cup of dry beans should yield approximately 2½ cups cooked beans.

Using a Slow Cooker

Slow cookers work well for recipes that call for simmering or roasting. To adjust recipes for the slow cooker, cut the liquid in half, since slow cookers retain moisture.

For recipes that call for 15 to 30 minutes in the oven or on the stovetop, food can be prepared in the slow cooker in 4 to 6 hours on the low setting or about 2 hours on the high setting.

For recipes that call for 35 to 45 minutes in the oven or on the stovetop, food can be prepared in the slow cooker in 6 to 8 hours on the low setting or about 3 to 4 hours on the high setting.

Baked Beans

This recipe starts with 2 cups of dry great northern or navy beans, cooked and drained. This will yield approximately 4 cups of cooked beans.

4 cups of great northern or navy beans, cooked and drained
¼ cup water
½ cup organic ketchup
½ cup Sucanat
¼ cup molasses

Combine ingredients in a pan and simmer over low heat. Serve warm.

WHITE BEAN AND SAGE PATTIES

1 cup white beans, soaked and cooked (makes approximately 2 cups of cooked beans)
1 small carrot, grated
1/3 cup yellow cornmeal
1 teaspoon fresh sage, chopped
Salt to taste
Ground black pepper to taste
Olive oil for sautéing
2 tablespoons water

Drain beans and mash. Stir in carrot, cornmeal and sage. Season with salt and pepper to taste. If mixture is too dry, add up to 2 tablespoons of water slowly. Form into small, 3-inch patties and sauté in a large skillet until golden brown and crisp, approximately 2 to 3 minutes on each side. Makes approximately 12 small patties.

WHITE BEAN AND ROASTED GARLIC DIP

The following is a wonderful dip to serve with pita wedges or chopped fresh vegetables.

1 garlic bulb, roasted
1 cup white beans, soaked and cooked (makes approximately 2 cups of cooked beans)
2 tablespoons lemon juice, freshly squeezed

Preheat oven to 375 degrees. Squeeze roasted garlic from cloves into food processor. Add beans and lemon juice and pulse until well blended.

TO ROAST BEETS

Preheat oven to 400 degrees. Cut off green stems and save them for another dish. Scrub beets well. Place beets in a baking dish and drizzle them with olive oil. Cover beets tightly with foil and roast for 1 hour and 15 minutes or until beets are fork tender. Let beets cool to touch and pull the peel from the beet. The beet will release its peel easily after roasting, but it gets very messy. Be careful of the beet's red juice and wear an apron and gloves if desired. Roasted beets can be eaten plain or in salads or used in other recipes.

Beet Bread

Since beets stain easily, clean up splatters quickly, wear an apron and wear gloves to prepare this bread.

2 large beets
½ cup milk
2¼ teaspoons active dry yeast
1 teaspoon sugar
¾ cup warm water
3½ to 4½ cups all-purpose flour
2 teaspoons salt
2 tablespoons olive oil

Peel beets and chop into small ¼-inch pieces. Puree in a food processor with ½ cup milk until mixture is free of lumps. This should make about 1½ cups of puree.

In small bowl, combine yeast, sugar, and water. Let rest for 5 minutes.

Combine flour and salt in a large bowl. Add in yeast mixture, beet puree and olive oil. Mix until just combined. Knead by hand or in a stand mixer equipped with a dough hook for about 10 minutes or until dough is smooth and elastic. Place dough in a lightly greased bowl. Cover and let rise until doubled, approximately 1 to 1½ hours.

Remove dough and shape into a round ball. Place on a baking stone or a parchment-lined baking sheet. Cover with a clean, dry towel and let rise until doubled, approximately 1 hour.

Make an X shape on the top of the loaf with a serrated knife and place in a 375-degree oven. Bake for 30 to 35 minutes or until a thermometer inserted reads 190 degrees. Allow bread to cool completely before slicing.

Beet Greens

Greens from approximately 4 beets
1 tablespoon olive oil
1 clove garlic, minced
Salt (optional)
Ground black pepper (optional)

Wash greens and tear them into small pieces. In a large pot over medium heat, heat oil and sauté garlic. Add beet leaves and a pinch of salt and pepper if desired. Sauté greens for approximately 5 minutes, stirring frequently. Cover pot and cook until tender.

> Despite their name, black-eyed peas are a bean, not a pea. To cook black-eyed peas, cover them with water in a large saucepan. Bring to a boil over high heat. Reduce heat to low and simmer, covered, until peas are soft when pierced with a fork. Drain and use.

Blueberry Oat Muffins

1 cup old-fashioned oats, uncooked
1 cup buttermilk
2 egg whites, lightly beaten
2 tablespoons butter, melted
½ teaspoon grated lemon peel
1 cup all-purpose flour
3 tablespoons sugar
1 teaspoon baking powder
½ teaspoon baking soda
¼ teaspoon salt
1 cup blueberries

Preheat oven to 400 degrees. Lightly coat muffin pan with oil or butter or use muffin liners. In medium bowl, mix oats and buttermilk. Let stand for 10 minutes. Add egg whites, butter and lemon peel. Mix until well blended. In a separate bowl, combine flour, sugar, baking powder, baking soda and salt. Mix well. Pour into buttermilk mixture and stir until just moistened. Gently fold in blueberries. Fill muffin cups until almost full. Bake for 20 to 25 minutes or until golden brown. Let cool at least 5 minutes before removing muffins from pan. Makes approximately 12 muffins.

> To prevent berries from sinking to the bottom of the pan, coat berries with flour before adding to batter.

Blueberry Sauce

2 cups fresh blueberries
1/4 cup sugar
1/4 cup water
1 tablespoon organic cornstarch
Dash nutmeg

Combine all ingredients in a saucepan and mix well. Cook over medium heat, stirring constantly, until mixture boils and thickens (approximately 5 to 7 minutes). Cool mixture. Serve over angel food cake, pancakes or waffles.

> To keep baking bread moist, put a small baking dish of water in the oven while the bread is baking.

Quick Bread Tips

Quick breads are generally made with leavening agents other than yeast. Quick breads include zucchini bread, banana bread, soda bread, beer bread, etc.

When making quick breads, mix wet ingredients into dry ingredients until just blended. Over mixing the batter will result in tough bread.

To keep the top of quick bread from cracking, rest the batter for approximately fifteen minutes before baking.

Quick breads freeze well. Allow breads to cool completely and wrap well before freezing.

Broccoli Cheese Soup

½ medium onion, chopped
1 tablespoon butter
¼ cup butter, melted
¼ cup flour
2 cups half and half
2 cups chicken broth
½ pound fresh broccoli, chopped fine
1 cup finely chopped carrots
8 ounces cheese, grated
Salt to taste
Ground pepper to taste

Sauté onion in 1 tablespoon butter and set aside. Cook melted butter and flour over medium heat for 3 to 5 minutes, stirring constantly. Continue to stir while adding half and half and broth. Simmer for 20 minutes. Add broccoli, onions and carrots and cook for 20 to 25 minutes. Add cheese and mix well. Season with salt and pepper to taste. Makes approximately 4 servings.

Roasted Brussels Sprouts

Preheat oven to 425 degrees. Trim whole sprouts at the base. Cut each sprout in half lengthwise and place in a rimmed baking dish. Coat well with olive oil and season lightly with salt. Cook until brown and tender, tossing occasionally, approximately 20 to 30 minutes. Serve with a drizzle of balsamic or apple cider vinegar or a sprinkle of Romano cheese.

Butter Cream Frosting

The following recipe was adapted from a recipe submitted by Shannon of Scrumptious. It can be used on her recipe for Lemon Tea Cakes.

1 cup butter, softened
2 tablespoons lemon zest
Lemon juice (tartness to liking)
1 teaspoon vanilla extract
4 cups confectioners sugar
2 tablespoons milk

In a large bowl, cream together the butter, lemon zest, lemon juice and vanilla. Blend in the sugar, one cup at a time, beating well after each addition. Beat in the milk and continue mixing until light and fluffy.

Tips for Baking a Moist Cake

Let cold ingredients come to room temperature.
Cream butter well.
Add egg whites last.
Preheat oven and do not let batter sit before baking.
Thinly frost while still warm.

Cabbage Slaw

½ head of red cabbage, thinly sliced
½ cup of organic mayonnaise
1 teaspoon white balsamic vinegar
¼ teaspoon ground black pepper
¼ teaspoon sea salt
⅛ teaspoon ground white pepper

Mix everything together in a bowl and serve cold.

Candied Flowers

This recipe for candied flowers was submitted by Shannon of Scrumptious.

Mint leaves or any edible flower, like pansies, violets, violas or roses
2 egg whites
2 teaspoons water
1 cup sugar
Cookie sheet for drying leaves and flowers
Small paint brush

Rinse flowers and leaves. Whip egg whites and water in a bowl. Cut enough flowers (blooms) or mint leaves for each cupcake. Brush flowers and leaves with egg whites with a small brush and coat both sides with sugar. Lay each out on a cookie sheet and let them harden. Arrange candied flowers on top of frosted cupcakes.

Caprese Salad

Mozzarella cheese
Tomatoes
Basil leaves
Olive oil
Salt and black pepper to taste

Slice mozzarella into thin pieces. Slice tomatoes. Arrange cheese, tomatoes and basil on a serving dish. Do this by either alternating each item in rows or in a design or place cheese on top of the tomatoes and sprinkle with basil. Drizzle olive oil and sprinkle salt and pepper over the items.

Other ingredients to consider trying in Caprese Salad include black olives, grated carrot, chopped garlic and balsamic vinegar.

Caramel Corn

This caramel corn recipe is great for the holidays.

1 cup organic sugar
¼ cup light corn syrup

6 tablespoons salted butter, melted
2 tablespoons water
2 teaspoons vanilla extract
½ teaspoon baking soda
10 cups popped popcorn
1 cup lightly salted peanuts (optional)

Preheat oven to 250 degrees. Line a rimmed baking sheet with parchment paper and set aside. In a small saucepan, whisk together the sugar, corn syrup, butter and water and bring to a simmer over medium-high heat. Continue to simmer, stirring often, until the mixture reaches 250 degrees on a candy thermometer, about 3 to 5 minutes. Turn off heat and whisk in vanilla and baking soda. Immediately pour the hot mixture over the popcorn. Use a rubber spatula to gently fold the caramel into the popcorn until coated. Gently stir in the peanuts and transfer the mixture to the prepared baking sheet, spreading it out. Bake for 1 hour, stirring every 20 minutes. Remove from the oven. Gently break up the popcorn. Store in an airtight container for up to 5 days.

Carrot Cake

1½ cups Sucanat or organic sugar
2 cups wheat flour
1½ teaspoons ground cinnamon
1 teaspoon baking soda
½ teaspoon salt
¼ teaspoon ground nutmeg
1 pound carrots
1 cup natural applesauce
3 eggs
2 tablespoons olive oil
1 teaspoon vanilla

Heat oven to 350 degrees. Lightly oil and flour an 8x11x5 pan. Mix dry ingredients together and set aside. Clean, peel and grate carrots. Blend carrots with applesauce, eggs, olive oil and vanilla. Add dry ingredients. Stir until well mixed.

Bake for 30 minutes or until a wooden toothpick inserted in the middle of cake comes out clean. Frost with cream cheese frosting if desired.

CARROT GINGER SOUP

2 pounds carrots, cleaned and peeled, cut into 1-inch pieces
4 cups stock or water
1–2 onions, chopped
2 garlic cloves
2 tablespoons fresh ginger
½ teaspoon cumin
Salt, to taste

Simmer carrots in water or stock until tender. In a fry pan, sauté onions until soft. Add garlic and ginger and cook until fragrant. Place carrots, including water or stock, sautéed onions and cumin in a food processor or blender and puree until smooth. Salt to taste and serve warm.

Add whole spices early in soups and stews or when fixing uncooked foods, such as juices, salad dressings and salads. Add ground herbs, spices and seeds just before food has finished cooking. Prolonged heat can destroy the flavors.

CARROT YOGURT SALAD

3 cups grated carrots
¼ cup sunflower seeds
1 cup vanilla yogurt
⅔ cup raisins
¼ teaspoon nutmeg

Combine carrots, sunflower seeds, yogurt and raisins in a bowl. Sprinkle nutmeg on top of salad. Makes approximately 6 servings

Cherries can easily be kept frozen and stored until needed for pies or other baked goods. Rinse cherries well and remove stems and pits.

Lay the cherries out in a single layer on a cookie sheet. Place cookie sheet in the freezer until individual cherries are frozen. Then take the cherries off the cookie sheet and place in freezer storage containers.

Mulled Cider

Preparing mulled cider in a slow cooker allows the spicy scent to drift through the house. Mulled cider is perfect for cold days and served with homemade cookies.

2 quarts apple cider
1/4 cup sucanat
2 sticks cinnamon
1 teaspoon whole cloves
1/8 teaspoon ground ginger
1 orange, sliced (unpeeled)

Combine everything in a slow-cooker. Cover and cook on low for 2 to 5 hours. Serve with a ladle straight from the slow cooker. Makes approximately 10 to 12 servings.

Coffee Butter Cream Frosting

This frosting is great on cakes and cupcakes, especially for those who love coffee. For an added touch, chocolate-covered espresso beans can be used for decorating.

1/2 cup butter, softened
3 cups powdered sugar
1 1/2 tablespoons strong brewed coffee
1/2 teaspoon vanilla
1 tablespoon milk, as needed

Cream butter in a bowl with an electric mixer. Slowly add sugar, coffee and vanilla. Mix until light and fluffy. If needed, add a little milk.

Cheese tastes best served at room temperature.

CHEESE MUFFINS

These cheese muffins are great with baked beans or chili.

1¼ cups all-purpose flour
½ cup coarse grind cornmeal
2½ teaspoons baking powder
½ teaspoon salt
2 eggs
1 cup milk
2 tablespoons butter, melted
1½ tablespoons honey
1½ cups grated Lock 21 cheese (or your favorite cheddar)

Preheat oven to 400 degrees. Oil muffin tins. Combine dry ingredients. In a separate bowl, combine eggs, milk, butter and honey. Stir dry and wet ingredients together quickly and add cheese. Fill muffin cups until they are about three-quarters full. Bake until muffins are slightly browned and springy, about 18 to 20 minutes. Makes approximately 10 to 12 muffins.

American cheese is processed with emulsifiers, preservatives and often food coloring. It holds together well and melts evenly. This is why it is often used on burgers and other grilled sandwiches. Some manufacturers add so much processed material to their American cheese that they can no longer call it cheese. They sell the products under different names such as cheese spread or cheese product.

CHICKEN STOCK

For making chicken stock, use the leftover bones and skin from a cooked or raw chicken carcass. Place all pieces in a slow cooker. Add whatever vegetables may be on hand or in season—celery, onions, carrots, etc.—and cover completely with water. Set slow cooker to high until water simmers. Turn on low and let cook for several hours or overnight. Let cool and remove bones; strain the stock into a container. Stock can be refrigerated or frozen for later use. After it cools, the stock may be gelatinous and, when heated, will become liquid again.

What Do the Labels on Chicken Packages Mean?

There are quite a few labels that can cause confusion. For example, some chicken is labeled hormone free. However, all chicken should be hormone free. Although hormones are used in cattle, the USDA prohibits the use of hormones in poultry.

All natural is one of the most widely used labels on chicken because it is an easy label to acquire. Natural simply means that no additives or preservatives were added after the chicken was processed. However, certain sodium-based broths may be added, so be sure to scan the fine print. The label says nothing about the standard of care, quality of feed or whether medication was used on the chicken before processing.

Raised without antibiotics simply indicates that, indeed, the chicken was raised without antibiotics for disease prevention or otherwise. However, medications that are not classified as antibiotics can still be used.

Farm raised is a label given to any producer raising chickens to sell. The USDA defines a farm as any operation that sells at least $1,000 of agricultural commodities, so almost any operation is entitled to use this label. In most cases, these farms are not the type people imagine, with red barns and happy chickens.

Free range chickens are granted access to the outdoors. But this may mean that the chickens are provided with as few as one small door in a huge warehouse where the chickens could go out if they decided to do so. In most cases, free range chickens do not get outdoors, even though a door is provided.

To have the **Certified Humane Raised and Handled** label, the chicken has received the basic standards of care set by the Society for the Prevention of Cruelty to Animals and the Humane Society of the United States. Producers must provide a sufficient quantity of fresh feed and continuous access to clean water, at least six continuous hours of darkness for every twenty-four-hour cycle and approximately a square foot of space for each chicken.

To have the **USDA-certified organic label**, all feed given to chickens must be certified organic. This means that no chemical fertilizers, pesticides, animal byproducts or other additives are in the feed.

Chive Butter Spread

This spread is great on corn or potatoes.

½ cup butter, softened
1 tablespoon fresh chives, chopped

Combine ingredients until well blended. Press into a serving dish and refrigerate if not using right away.

Chocolate Pudding

⅔ cup evaporated cane juice
3 tablespoons unsweetened cocoa powder
¼ cup organic cornstarch
⅛ teaspoon salt
3 cups milk
1 teaspoon vanilla extract

In a medium saucepan, combine evaporated cane juice, cocoa powder, cornstarch and salt. Pour in milk and whisk together. Stir over medium-high heat until mixture starts to boil. Turn heat down slightly and continue to stir while cooking until thick, approximately 5 minutes. Take off heat and stir in vanilla. Allow pudding to cool for 10 minutes before serving warm. Or refrigerate and serve chilled. Makes approximately 6 servings.

While warm, chocolate pudding can be poured into a 9-inch pie pan and chocolate pie crust to make a pudding pie.

Coffee Custard

3 egg yolks
½ cup sugar
1 tablespoon all-purpose flour
1 teaspoon vanilla extract
1 shot (approximately 1 to 1½ ounces) strong espresso, at room temperature
¼ cup milk
1 cup heavy whipping cream

In a small saucepan, combine egg yolks, sugar, flour, vanilla and espresso and mix until combined. Place on a stove over medium heat. Add milk a little at a time, stirring constantly. Bring to a boil and reduce to a simmer, continuing to stir until mixture thickens. Remove from heat and let cool. In a separate bowl, mix the cream until it forms a thick whipped cream. Gently fold ⅔ of whipped cream into the custard mix. Separate custard into 6 dessert dishes and place in refrigerator for approximately 1 hour. Top custard with remaining whipped cream just before serving.

Uses for Used Coffee Grounds

Put used coffee grounds in the compost. They are a valuable source of nitrogen.

Work used coffee grounds into garden soil. Coffee grounds are said to repel ants, snails and slugs, as well as add nitrogen to the soil. Used coffee grounds are great for plants that thrive in acidic soil, such as azaleas and blueberries. Used coffee grounds can also be used to mulch plants that slugs like to eat, such as lilies and hostas.

Place a container of used coffee grounds in the refrigerator or freezer to absorb odors. A few drops of vanilla can also be added to the coffee grounds. Change out the container when the grounds become too moist or start to lose their own odor.

Rub used coffee grounds on hands to get rid of smells from chopping pungent foods.

Soak cutting boards with used coffee grounds to help remove food odors.

Corn on the Cob

This simple way to cook corn on the cob helps the corn come out sweet and tender.

Shuck corn and remove silk right before cooking. Place corn in a large pot with just enough cold water to cover corn. Add approximately 1 tablespoon of sugar for each gallon of water in the pot. Bring water to a boil and boil for 2 minutes. Remove from heat and let corn sit in the water for 10 minutes. Drain water and serve.

Corn Tomato Salad

6 ears corn, husked and cleaned
1 tomato, diced
1 green pepper, diced
½ red onion, diced
¼ cup olive oil
⅓ cup vinegar
1 tablespoon minced garlic

Cut corn off cob and mix corn with diced tomato, green pepper and onion. Cover with olive oil, vinegar and minced garlic. Mix well.

Cream Cheese Frosting

This recipe was submitted by Shannon of Scrumptious. It can be used with her recipe for Fruit Pizza or on any cupcakes or cakes.

3 cups powdered sugar
1 package (8 ounces) cream cheese, softened
¼ cup butter, softened
2 tablespoons milk
1 teaspoon vanilla

In a large bowl, stir all frosting ingredients until smooth.

Garlic Butter Croutons

This recipe for croutons is a great way to use up leftover bread.

6 tablespoons butter
2 cloves garlic, peeled and smashed
Bread, approximately 4 slices cut into small cubes (will make about 4 cups)
Sea salt

Preheat oven to 350 degrees. Melt butter in a small saucepan over low heat. Add garlic and cook until butter is fragrant, approximately 3 to 4 minutes. Remove from heat and remove garlic from butter. Evenly coat bread cubes with butter and spread on a rimmed baking sheet. Sprinkle lightly with salt and place pan in center of oven. Bake until croutons are a deep golden brown, approximately 15 minutes. Let cool. Store croutons in a sealed container for up to 2 days in the refrigerator.

Cucumber and Black-Eyed Pea Salad

3 tablespoons olive oil
2 tablespoons lemon juice
2 teaspoons chopped fresh oregano
4 cups peeled and diced cucumbers
15 ounces cooked black-eyed peas
½ cup crumbled feta cheese
¼ cup diced red onion
2 tablespoons chopped black olives

In large bowl, whisk together olive oil, lemon juice and oregano. Add cucumber, black-eyed peas, feta cheese, onion and olives. Mix well. Serve at room temperature or chilled.

PASTA SAUCE WITH EGGPLANT

This recipe was submitted by Pam Weirauch of Pam's Corner, Ltd., in Toledo.

1 small onion, finely chopped
½ cup sliced mushrooms
2 cloves crushed garlic
1 tablespoon olive oil
¼ cup chopped celery
1 cup cubed eggplant, unpeeled
½ cup diced red pepper
½ cup dry white wine
Pinch nutmeg
3 cups coarsely chopped Roma tomatoes
1 teaspoon chopped fresh basil (or ½ teaspoon dried basil)
5 cups of your favorite cooked pasta

Sauté onion, mushroom and garlic in oil. Add celery, eggplant and red pepper and sauté about 2 additional minutes. Add remaining ingredients for sauce and bring to a slow boil, then lower heat to simmer. Cook uncovered over medium heat for 25 to 35 minutes. Serve hot over pasta. Serves 4 to 6.

EGGS

Before refrigeration, eggs were collected and stored on the counter or in the root cellar or basement. Eggs straight from the chicken have a coating, or bloom, over the egg. This bloom gives the egg's porous shell a protective coating. However, in commercial egg factories, this bloom is washed off, leaving the egg unprotected.

Eggs are a natural source of protein and many vitamins and minerals essential to good health. For several years, many people limited their consumption of eggs due to their cholesterol content. Studies now show that cholesterol in foods does not contribute significantly toward overall cholesterol levels, and eggs are making a comeback.[61]

Some cooks swear that farm fresh eggs from local farmers make better baked goods. The color of the egg has nothing to do with the flavor or the nutritional value of the egg. However, the diet and health of the chicken do make a difference.

Hard-boiled Eggs

There are different methods for making hard-boiled eggs. Cookbooks from the late 1800s reveal that, even then, every cook had a different take on how to hard boil eggs. Here is just one of many methods that creates a tender hard-boiled egg without the green ring around the yolk.

Bring a saucepan of water to a boil. Carefully add eggs with a slotted spoon. (Make sure the eggs are completely covered by water.) Let water come back to a boil for 1 minute. Turn off heat and cover pan. Let pan sit for 15 to 17 minutes, depending on the size of the egg. If serving cold, immediately rinse eggs under cold water and let them sit in cold water for several minutes.

Dying Eggs the Natural Way

Use fruits and vegetables to dye hard-boiled eggs the natural way. Preparing the egg dye takes longer than using artificial color tablets, but the results are worth it. It will take a bit longer for the dye to set on the eggs, too—anywhere from 5 to 15 minutes, depending on the desired darkness of the color.

Pink

1 large beet, washed and sliced
2 cups water
1 tablespoon vinegar

Bring beet slices and water to a boil and let simmer for at least 5 minutes. Strain beet water into a small dish that will be used to dip eggs into. Cool and stir in vinegar.

Blue

2 cups blueberries
2 cups water
1 tablespoon vinegar

Bring blueberries and water to a boil and let simmer for at least 5 minutes. Strain blueberry water into a small dish that will be used to dip eggs into. Cool and stir in vinegar.

WHAT DO THE LABELS ON EGG CARTONS MEAN?

Certified Organic eggs means the hens are fed an organic feed free of animal byproducts and antibiotics. Most of the hens are kept in large warehouses with limited access to the outdoors.

Vegetarian-Fed simply indicates that the hens eat feed that does not contain animal byproducts.

Omega-3 Enriched eggs come from hens consuming feed enriched with omega-3 foods, such as flaxseed, fishmeal or algae.

Natural is a marketing term used freely by producers. It has nothing to do with the quality of the egg or the hen that laid it.

There are no specifications for **Free Range** eggs. It typically means that hens are not caged and have some degree of access to the outdoors, but there are no requirements for the quality of access or amount of time they are allowed outside.

Certified Humane is a label provided through the Humane Farm Animal Care. The hens are not caged but kept indoors at all times. They must be able to nest, perch and dust bathe. Despite the Certified Humane label, there are no restrictions on beak trimming.

United Egg Producers Certified gives minimal guidelines on the care of chickens and is verified by the United Egg Producers. Although forced molting is not allowed, there are no restrictions on beak trimming. Chickens are given only sixty-seven square inches of cage space, which is less area than a sheet of paper.

American Humane Certified is a label verified through the American Humane Association. Hens can be either cage-free or confined. If confined, cages are extremely small. The American Humane Certified label does not put restrictions on beak trimming.

Fertile eggs simply mean they come from hens housed with roosters.

Breakfast Burritos

Breakfast burritos are a quick and easy item to make any time of day. They simply consist of wrapping scrambled eggs and cheese—and any other filling desired, such as vegetables and meat—in a tortilla.

Do not forget breakfast for dinner. Eggs, waffles, pancakes, French toast, breakfast burritos and more can be incorporated into evening meals. Add seasonal vegetables as fillings for breakfast burritos. Add seasonal fruits to waffle and pancake batter, make fruit topping or use fruit spreads found at the market.

Broccoli Cheese Potatoes

6 medium baking potatoes
½ cup sour cream
3 tablespoons butter
½ teaspoon salt
¼ teaspoon pepper
2 green onions
1½ cups broccoli, cooked and chopped
1 cup grated cheddar cheese
Paprika

Bake potatoes at 425 degrees for 45 to 60 minutes. Cut potatoes lengthwise. Scoop out pulp and place in a large bowl. Mash potatoes. Add sour cream, butter, salt, pepper, onions, broccoli and ¾ cup cheese. Refill potato shells, top with remaining cheese and sprinkle with paprika. Place back in the oven and bake at 425 degrees for 20 to 25 minutes or until heated through.

FRUIT CREAM PUFFS

These cream puffs are low in sugar. Seasonal fruit or fruit that has been frozen without added sugar can be used to make these delicious treats.

½ cup butter
1 cup water
1 cup all-purpose flour
4 eggs

Filling
1 cup cold whipping cream
1 teaspoon sugar
½ teaspoon vanilla extract
½ cup fresh fruit

Preheat oven to 400 degrees. In a medium saucepan, combine butter and water. Bring to boil and add flour. Stir together and continue to cook until mixture forms a dough. Remove from heat and allow to cool for about 10 minutes. Add eggs and beat with a spatula or spoon until smooth. Drop batter by heaping tablespoons onto a greased or lined baking sheet and bake for 20 to 25 minutes, or until lightly browned. Turn oven off. Remove from oven and, with a sharp knife, cut a 1- to 2-inch-long slit into each pastry puff. Place back in oven for approximately 5 minutes to help centers of pastry dry out. Remove and let cool.

To create filling, start with pouring whipping cream into a mixing bowl. Beat the cream with an electric mixer until soft peaks form. Add vanilla and sugar and whip until blended. Add fruit and blend lightly until well mixed. Open each cream puff and stuff each with filling. Serve immediately. Makes about 20 stuffed cream puffs.

Fruit Crisp

This is a handy and fast dessert that is made with fruit that has been canned in sweet syrup. This can also be made with any fruit that is on hand—apples, peaches, etc.

3 cups fruit that has been preserved in sweet syrup
¾ cup Sucanat
⅔ cup flour
½ cup rolled oats
¼ teaspoon salt
1 teaspoon cinnamon
6 tablespoons butter, cut into small chunks

Preheat oven to 425 degrees. Scoop fruit into the bottom of a 9-inch square baking dish. In a mixing bowl, combine dry ingredients. Add chunks of butter and mix well. Mixture will be a bit crumbly. Evenly spread crumbly mixture over the top of the fruit. Bake for 25 to 30 minutes or until topping is slightly browned.

Fruit Granola Bars

This delicious granola bar recipe can be made with several different fruit spreads offered by vendors at the market.

2 cups uncooked rolled oats
1 cup flour
½ teaspoon baking soda
¾ cup butter
⅓ cup Sucanat
½ teaspoon salt
10 ounces of fruit spread

Preheat oven to 350 degrees and coat an 8x10-inch baking dish with butter. Combine oats, flour, baking soda, butter, Sucanat and salt in a mixing bowl. When thoroughly combined, take out ¾ cup of the mixture and set aside. Press remaining mixture into the bottom of the baking dish. Bake for 10 minutes. Spread fruit over top and sprinkle with ¾ cup oat mixture. Bake an additional 20 minutes or until lightly browned.

Fruit Yogurt Freezer Pops

Making refreshing freezer treats is easy. Blend together equal amounts of vanilla yogurt and any fruit. Pour mixture into freezer pop molds and freeze until hard.

> Use overripe fruit in smoothies or puree and add to baked goods.

Fruit Pizza

This recipe was submitted by Shannon of Scrumptious. It is one of the favorites among her customers, friends and family. The fruit pizza can change with the seasons. Start out with a favorite sugar cookie recipe or the one provided by Shannon for the crust.

<u>Sugar Cookie Crust</u>
1½ cups butter
2¼ cups white sugar
3 eggs
1 teaspoon vanilla extract
9 cups all-purpose flour
2 teaspoons baking powder
1 teaspoon baking soda
3 cups milk
Seasonal fruit, washed and sliced as desired

Preheat oven to 350 degrees. In a large bowl, cream together the butter and sugar until light and fluffy. Add the eggs one at a time, beating well with each addition. Stir in the vanilla. Combine the flour, baking powder and baking soda in a separate bowl. Stir flour mixture into the cream mixture alternately with milk. Press into the bottom of a greased cookie or cake pan. Baking time depends on the size of the cookie crust made, usually about 15 minutes. (Baked cookie crust can also be frozen for later use.)

Frost the cookie crust all the way to the edges with cream cheese frosting. Arrange seasonal fruits on top of frosted cookie crust. Refrigerate until ready to serve.

Roasted Garlic

Fresh garlic bulbs, any amount
Olive oil

Preheat oven to 375 degrees. Cut about ¼ inch from the top of the garlic bulb. Place garlic in a garlic baker or on a sheet of foil. Drizzle a small amount of olive oil over bulb. Cover garlic baker or, if using foil, wrap foil around bulb until it is sealed inside, then place foil package in a baking dish. Place garlic in oven and bake until soft, about 30 minutes. Remove garlic from oven and let cool to room temperature. Garlic can now be easily squeezed from the skins.

Gluten-Free Flour Mix

4 cups superfine brown rice flour
1⅓ cups potato starch
⅔ cup tapioca flour

Mix together well and use the amount of flour needed in recipes for a gluten-free alternative. Keep unused amount stored in a sealed container.

Green Salsa

This recipe was submitted by Lindsay Graham of Omega Meats, near Grand Rapids.

½ cup tomatillos, diced
½ cup scallions, minced
1½ tablespoons garlic, finely chopped
⅓ cup poblano, finely chopped
½ cup cilantro, coarsely chopped
2 tablespoons lime juice
½ teaspoon salt
2 tablespoons water

Mix all ingredients together and serve.

HERBAL VINEGARS

Herbal vinegars can be added to soups and used as salad dressings and marinades for meat and vegetables. Herbal vinegars are relatively easy to make. Just add four cups of vinegar to one cup of any herb and let sit in a dark cupboard for two to four weeks.

The purple blossoms of chives make a stunningly pink herbal vinegar while the blossoms fade to white inside the bottle of vinegar.

Opal basil creates a visually appealing red herbal vinegar.

HERBED PASTA

1 pound whole wheat farfalle pasta
1 tablespoon olive oil
1½ tablespoons chives, chopped
1½ tablespoons basil, chopped
1½ tablespoons dill, chopped
1 cup plain yogurt
¼ cup chopped sundried tomatoes
½ teaspoon salt
½ teaspoon pepper
¾ cup shredded parmesan cheese

In a large saucepan, cook pasta in water according to directions on package. Drain and rinse pasta and return it to saucepan. Add olive oil, herbs, yogurt, sundried tomatoes, salt and pepper. Reheat over low heat, stirring frequently. (Do not overheat.)

After heating thoroughly, remove from heat and fold in parmesan cheese. Serve warm. If serving cold, simply mix all of the ingredients with prepared cold noodles.

HONEY

When replacing sugar with honey in recipes, use ½ cup honey to 1 cup sugar and reduce the amount of liquid in the recipe by ¼ cup for each cup of honey added. Adding ½ teaspoon of baking soda for each cup of honey used will help the food rise. Also, reduce the oven temperature by 25 degrees to prevent overbaking.

If honey crystallizes, immerse jar in hot water.

Honey Cream Cheese Frosting

½ cup butter, softened
8 ounces cream cheese
¼ cup honey
1 teaspoon cinnamon

In a medium bowl, mix all ingredients until smooth.

Honey is a terrific soother for sore throats. To create a soothing syrup, thoroughly mix honey with the juice squeezed from a lemon. Drink the solution to coat the throat.

Vanilla Ice Cream

2 egg yolks
2/3 cup evaporated cane juice
2 cups milk
1 cup cream
1 teaspoon vanilla extract

Combine egg yolks, evaporated cane juice and milk in a medium saucepan. Stir constantly over low heat. Heat until small bubbles appear on the edges of mixture, to approximately 175 degrees. Take off heat, cover and chill. Add cream and vanilla. Whisk until combined. Prepare in an ice cream maker according to directions in the manual.

Lemon Tea Cakes

This recipe was submitted by Shannon of Scrumptious. These teacakes are very popular for Mother's Day and garden weddings.

2 cups flour
2 teaspoons baking powder
1 tablespoon cornstarch
1 teaspoon salt
6 tablespoons butter
1½ cups white sugar
3 eggs
4 egg yolks, beaten
1 teaspoon vanilla extract
1 cup milk
1½ cups fresh lemon juice
1 tablespoon grated lemon zest

Preheat oven to 350 degrees. Line muffin pan with cupcake papers. In a mixing bowl, combine flour, baking powder, cornstarch and salt. In a separate large bowl, cream together the butter and sugar until light and fluffy, about 5 minutes. Beat in the eggs and egg yolks one at a time and then stir in the vanilla. Beat in the flour mixture alternately with the milk. Add lemon juice and lemon zest and mix just until incorporated. Pour batter into prepared pans. Bake in the preheated oven for 12 to 15 minutes, or until a toothpick inserted into the center of the teacakes comes out clean. Allow to cool.

Spread butter cream frosting on each teacake and decorate with candied flowers and mint leaves.

Maple Dressing

This easy-to-make dressing is perfect on baby greens.

¾ cup pure maple syrup
½ cup natural rice vinegar
1 teaspoon salt
1 large clove garlic, minced

1½ teaspoons ground mustard
1 cup extra-virgin olive oil

Combine all ingredients in a blender. Blend until smooth and serve at room temperature. Store unused dressing in a sealed container in the refrigerator.

Panzanella

1 loaf crusty bread
5 medium tomatoes, cut into chunks
2 cloves garlic, minced
¼ cup balsamic vinegar
¼ cup basil, chopped fine
3 medium-size balls of fresh mozzarella, cut into bite-size pieces
Olive oil to taste
Salt to taste
Ground pepper to taste

Cut bread into 1-inch cubes and broil in oven until toasted. Set aside and let cool. Combine tomatoes, garlic, balsamic vinegar, basil and mozzarella in a large bowl. Drizzle with olive oil and add salt and pepper to taste. Add bread cubes right before serving to prevent them from getting soggy. Serves 6.

Maple-Roasted Parsnips

These maple-roasted parsnips would go well as a side dish with pot roast or are fantastic on their own.

2½ pounds parsnips
½ cup olive oil
½ cup pure maple syrup
Salt to taste
Ground pepper to taste

Preheat oven to 400 degrees. Clean and peel parsnips. Cut each parsnip in half lengthwise. Take each half and cut into quarters lengthwise. Place parsnips in a baking dish and cover well with olive oil. Pour maple syrup over the oil-covered parsnips and place in oven. Roast for 35 minutes or until they are tender and golden brown. Salt and pepper to taste.

Peaches

Most peaches sold in stores and markets are called freestone. Freestone simply means the flesh of the peach will come cleanly from the stone, or seed, of the peach. Freestone varieties are excellent for slicing for use in salads and canning.

If the peach is a cling variety, the flesh will cling to the stone, making removal of the stone more difficult. Cling peaches are rarely found in stores, so they are a special local treat when available. They are great for eating fresh and for making jams and preserves.

To soften peaches, place them in a single layer in a loosely closed paper bag for a day or two.

Ripe peaches can be stored in the refrigerator for a week.

Ripe peaches can be peeled for cooking or baking by placing them in a pot full of boiling water for about thirty seconds. They should be in the water just long enough to loosen the skin, not cook the peach. The peaches should then be transferred to a bowl full of ice water for approximately two minutes. Now the skins should slip off easily.

Grilled Peaches

2 tablespoons butter
2 tablespoons organic sugar
1 teaspoon ground cinnamon
2 tablespoons honey
3 freestone peaches, pitted and halved

In a small saucepan, melt butter. Add sugar, cinnamon and honey and stir until melted. Remove from heat.

Cut each peach in half and remove stone. Heat grill to medium heat. Make sure grates are clean and brushed with oil. Brush cut side of peach with butter. Place cut side down on grill and grill until slightly soft. Remove peaches and place on serving plates. Drizzle honey mixture over grilled peaches. Serve warm and with a side of vanilla ice cream if desired.

Refrigerator Pickles

The following recipe will make approximately two quart jars of pickles. Do not use copper, brass, galvanized or iron pots or cooking utensils. These metals can react with the acids in pickles.

Brine
3 cups distilled water
1 cup distilled white vinegar
2 tablespoons kosher, non-iodized salt

Place the following in each jar:
Cucumbers
½ teaspoon dried garlic, minced
¼ teaspoon yellow mustard seed
2 black peppercorns
2 whole allspice
½ teaspoon dried cayenne pepper
Pinch of dill seed
Pinch of dill weed
Pinch of turmeric
¼ teaspoon sugar

Place water, vinegar and salt in a glass saucepan and bring mixture to a boil. Pour over the cucumbers and spices in jars and seal. Store in refrigerator. Pickles will be ready in 7 to 10 days and will keep for up to 4 months.

Chocolate Pie Crust

This pie crust is great for pies that call for chocolate cookie crusts. It will work for a single 9-inch pie.

7 tablespoons butter, softened
⅓ cup evaporated cane juice
1¼ cup all-purpose flour
¼ cup unsweetened organic cocoa powder
1 egg, beaten

Stir all ingredients together and mix until dough forms. Place dough in center of pie plate and, using fingers, pat the dough down and up the sides of the pie plate. Either pinch the edges of the dough to make a design or trim excess flush with the edge of the pie plate. If the recipe requires a prebaked crust, preheat oven to 425 degrees. Poke the bottom of the crust a couple times with a fork to keep air bubbles from forming and bake for 10 minutes.

The easiest way to make pie crust is in a food processor. However, it can also be done by hand. Simply use a fork and a knife to cut the butter into the dry ingredients.

DOUBLE PIE CRUST

The following recipe can be used for pies requiring a double crust, such as blueberry and apple pies.

2½ cups all-purpose flour, plus extra for rolling
1 teaspoon salt
1 teaspoon sugar
½ cup butter, very cold
6 tablespoons cold water

Combine flour, salt and sugar in a food processor. Pulse to mix. Add butter and pulse until mixture resembles coarse meal with small, pea-sized pieces of butter. Add cold water 1 tablespoon at a time, pulsing until mixture just begins to clump together. Continue to add water until dough holds together. Place dough on a clean surface and shape into two discs. Do not over handle dough. Small chunks of butter in the crust is fine and will create a flaky crust. On a lightly floured surface, roll the first disc out into a 12-inch circle with a rolling pin. (Dough will be about 1/8 inch thick.) Fold dough into quarters and place in 9-inch pie pan with the point in the center of the pan. Unfold and ease the dough into the pan.

Add filling to the pie. Roll out the second disc as before and gently place on top of the filling in the pie. Pinch the edges of the top and bottom crusts together. Trim extra dough off the edges and flute edges with thumb and forefinger or press with a fork. Score the top of the pie with four 2-inch long cuts so steam can escape from the pie while cooking.

How to Make a Lattice Crust

To create a pie with the look of lattice, roll out the top dough so that when cut, the dough will be long enough to cover the pie, including a bit of overhang. Using a pastry wheel or pizza cutter, cut strips of dough as wide or as narrow as desired. Lay down the center vertical strips on the pie and work outward from the center, spacing the strips as desired. Fold back every other strip halfway and lay a strip down the center horizontally. Unfold the strips and fold back the opposite strips. Lay another strip horizontally and continue to repeat this step for the rest of the pie. Trim any excess and press down the ends into the bottom edge of the crust.

Graham Cracker Pie Crust

This recipe was submitted by Ackerman's Berry Farm. The graham cracker crust is perfect with its recipe for Fresh Raspberry Pie. The easiest way to make graham cracker crumbs is to place whole crackers in the blender or food processor and pulse them until they are crumbs.

1½ cups graham cracker crumbs
1 tablespoon brown sugar
6 tablespoons melted butter

Mix the crumbs and brown sugar together. Add melted butter and stir to combine. Press mixture into a 9-inch pie plate and bake at 350 degrees for 10 minutes.

PAT-IN-PAN PIE CRUST

This pie crust recipe was adapted from one submitted by Lynne Weiland. This is a wonderfully easy pie crust for a single 8- or 9-inch pie.

1½ cups all-purpose flour
1½ teaspoons sugar
½ teaspoon salt
½ cup butter, softened
2 tablespoons milk

If the recipe requires a prebaked crust, preheat oven to 425 degrees. Place flour, sugar and salt in a small bowl and mix well. In a measuring cup, combine butter and milk and mix until blended. Pour into the bowl with the flour mixture and mix with a fork until completely moistened. Transfer the dough into the pie plate and, using fingers, pat the dough down and up the sides of the pie plate. Either pinch the edges of the dough to make a design or trim excess flush with the edge of the pie plate. Poke the bottom of the crust a couple times with a fork to keep air bubbles from forming and bake for 15 minutes.

> Unbaked pie crusts can be frozen for up to two months or kept in the refrigerator for up to three days.

POLENTA POUND CAKE

This cake is terrific alone or topped with fresh fruit or fruit compote.

½ cup butter
1 cup evaporated cane juice
Zest of one lemon, finely grated
3 eggs, at room temperature
1 teaspoon vanilla extract
½ cup plain yogurt
½ cup plus 2 tablespoons cornmeal
1 cup all-purpose flour

½ teaspoon baking powder
¼ teaspoon salt

Preheat oven to 350 degrees. Coat loaf pan with butter. Cream butter, evaporated cane juice and lemon zest until fluffy. Add eggs one at a time. Add vanilla extract and yogurt. Add cornmeal and mix well. In a separate bowl, combine flour, baking powder and salt. Pour flour mixture into cornmeal mixture and mix well. Pour batter into loaf pan and smooth out top with a spoon. Gently tap the pan on the counter to release any air pockets in the batter. Bake in the center of the oven for 60 minutes or until the top is golden brown and a toothpick comes out clean. Let cool for 10 minutes and serve warm.

Baked Potato Wedges

For this recipe, use salt and other spices—garlic powder, onion powder, chili powder, paprika or one of the great seasoning blends sold at the market.

2 large potatoes
1 teaspoon olive oil

Preheat oven to 400 degrees. Cut potatoes into quarters lengthwise and cut each quarter into a wedge. Lightly sprinkle wedges with seasoning of your choice. Lightly coat a cookie sheet or a large baking dish with olive oil. Lay wedges on the pan and place on the oven rack about 7 inches from the bottom of the oven. Bake for about 7 minutes or until the bottom and edges start browning. Turn wedges over to the other side and bake for another 7 minutes or until wedges are cooked throughout. Makes approximately 4 servings.

Mashed Potatoes

Wash potatoes thoroughly and, if desired, peel. Cut potatoes into equal-sized pieces and cook in water just until pieces are tender. Remove from heat and drain. Mash with a potato masher or with an electric mixer. Be sure not to over mix or potatoes will be sticky. Add one tablespoon of butter for each potato and salt to taste. Add enough milk to make the potatoes smooth and fluffy.

Most root vegetables—such as sweet potatoes, parsnips and carrots—are great additions to combine with potatoes in mashed potatoes. Use what is in season, cook and mash together.

Herbs can give mashed potatoes an interesting flavor. Chop herbs and gently fold into mashed potatoes.

Leftover mashed potatoes make a great thickener for soups, stews and sauces.

To keep peeled potatoes from browning, place them in a bowl of cold water until they are ready to be used.

MOIST PUMPKIN SQUARES

Fall ushers in cooler weather and squash of many different sizes and colors. The following recipe for Pumpkin Squares makes a superb, moist cake that tastes similar to pumpkin pie. The following recipe was adapted from a recipe from Egg & Honey.

2 cups flour
1 teaspoon baking powder
1 teaspoon salt
2 teaspoons cinnamon
½ teaspoon ginger
½ teaspoon ground cloves
1 cup applesauce
2 cups Sucanat (or 1 cup sugar and 1 cup brown sugar)
4 eggs, beaten
2 cups pureed pumpkin

Preheat oven to 350 degrees. Grease a 9x13 pan. Mix dry ingredients and set aside. In a separate bowl, stir together applesauce and sugars. Mix in eggs and pumpkin. Add dry ingredients. Smooth into pan and bake for 30 minutes or until a toothpick inserted in center comes out clean. Let cool and cut into small squares.

Baked Oatmeal

2 cups rolled oats
1/3 cup sugar
1 teaspoon baking powder
1 1/2 teaspoons ground cinnamon
1/2 teaspoon salt
2 cups milk
1 egg
3 tablespoons butter, melted
2 teaspoons pure vanilla extract
2 cups blueberries, strawberries or mixed berries

Preheat oven to 375 degrees. Butter an 8-inch square baking dish. In a bowl, combine oats, sugar, baking powder, cinnamon and salt. In a separate bowl, whisk together milk, egg, butter and vanilla. Arrange half of berries on the bottom of the coated baking dish. Cover berries with oat mixture, then pour the milk mixture over the oats. Sprinkle remaining berries across the top. Bake for 35 to 40 minutes or until the top is slightly browned. Serve warm.

Soaking Grains

Soaking whole grains, such as whole wheat, oats, kamut, spelt and brown rice, can neutralize phytic acid, break down complex starches and make grains easier to digest. It also softens the grains, and baked goods will have a lighter texture.

To soak grains effectively, 1 tablespoon of an acidic medium such as lemon juice, cultured buttermilk, milk kefir, cultured yogurt, whey or apple cider vinegar should be used per cup of water called for in the recipe. If used, dairy products must be cultured. If grains are not sufficiently soaked, liquid oil and sweeteners, such as honey, called for in the recipe can be added to the mixture. The liquids used should be warm.

Soak brown rice, buckwheat and millet for approximately 7 hours. All other grains—whole wheat, spelt, kamut, oats, barley, etc.—should be soaked for 12 to 24 hours. The grains can be left soaking at room temperature on the counter in a covered container. After soaking, add the remaining ingredients and proceed with the recipe.

Baked Cheese Quesadillas

Quesadillas make great easy and fast meals. Simply place shredded cheese on one side of a tortilla, fold and place on a baking sheet. Bake at 400 degrees for approximately 10 minutes or until tortilla is golden and crispy. Turn quesadilla with a large spatula once midway through baking time. Quesadillas can be cut into triangular shapes and served warm with salsa or sour cream if desired.

Baked quesadillas are great for seasonal vegetables, too. Simply dice up vegetables—peppers, tomatoes and more—and add to shredded cheese before baking.

Raspberry Iced Tea

2 cups brewed tea
2 cups raspberry juice
¼ cup honey

Mix tea, raspberries and honey together and stir until honey is dissolved. Serve cold over ice.

Fresh Raspberry Pie

This recipe was submitted by Ackerman's Berry Farm. This delicious pie can be made using their recipe for graham cracker crust.

1 cup raspberries, pureed
1 cup water
1 cup sugar
3 tablespoons cornstarch

4 cups fresh raspberries, whole
Graham cracker pie crust

In a medium saucepan, combine puree, water, sugar and cornstarch. Mix well. Bring mixture to a boil over medium-high heat and stir constantly until mixture boils and thickens. Pour 2 cups fresh raspberries in prepared pie crust and top with half of the warm glaze mixture. Add the remaining berries and then slowly add the remaining glaze. Refrigerate at least 4 hours before serving.

Raspberry Vinaigrette

¼ cup raspberry preserves
¼ cup balsamic vinegar
½ cup olive oil

Mix ingredients together and serve on a salad.

Rhubarb Cookies

1 cup butter
1½ cups brown sugar
2 eggs
3 cups all-purpose flour
1 teaspoon baking soda
½ teaspoon salt
1½ cups fresh rhubarb, diced

In a large mixing bowl, cream butter and brown sugar. Beat in eggs. In a separate bowl, combine flour, baking soda and salt. Add to cream mixture and stir until combined, then stir in the rhubarb. Drop batter by tablespoons, two inches apart, onto greased cookie sheets. Bake at 350 degrees for 12 to 15 minutes or until lightly browned. Cool and spread with cream cheese frosting if desired.

Rhubarb Brown Betty

This recipe was adapted from a recipe submitted by Lynne Weiland. The great thing about this recipe is that any bread on hand or leftover rolls from an evening meal can be used.

2 cups breadcrumbs
3 cups rhubarb, cut small
½ cup honey
¼ cup water
½ teaspoon nutmeg
3 tablespoons butter

Rub the inside of a deep baking dish generously with butter. Mix half of breadcrumbs and half of cut rhubarb in dish. In a separate saucepan, bring honey and water to a boil. Pour over breadcrumbs and rhubarb in the dish. Sprinkle nutmeg over the mixture, then dot with butter. Arrange the remaining rhubarb on top of the mixture. Place remaining breadcrumbs on top. Bake at 350 degrees for 30 to 40 minutes.

Rhubarb Custard Pie

This recipe was submitted by Lynne Weiland.

<u>Filling</u>
2 tablespoons flour
2 eggs
1 cup sugar
¾ cup cream
1½ cups rhubarb, diced
Unbaked 9-inch pie crust

Preheat oven to 350 degrees. In a large bowl, mix together all ingredients for filling except the rhubarb. Place rhubarb in an unbaked pie crust and pour mixture over it. Bake at 350 degrees for 45 minutes or until filling is set.

Spinach Egg Bake

4 eggs
1/3 cup milk
1/3 cup cheese (cheddar or your favorite), grated
1/3 cup fresh spinach, chopped
Dash of salt

Mix ingredients together and pour into a buttered loaf pan. Bake at 350 degrees for 30 minutes or until a knife inserted in the middle comes out clean. Makes approximately 3 small servings.

Strawberries have a high moisture content, so they should be stored uncovered or loosely covered. Rinse strawberries just before serving.

Strawberry Bread

This recipe was submitted by Whittaker's Berry Farm in Ida, Michigan.

3 eggs
2 cups sugar
1 cup olive oil
1 tablespoon vanilla
2 cups flour
1 cup quick oats
1 tablespoon cinnamon
1 teaspoon baking soda
1 teaspoon salt
½ teaspoon baking powder
2 cups crushed strawberries

Courtesy of Eleanor Billau.

Beat eggs and sugar. Add oil and vanilla. Mix in flour, oats, cinnamon, baking soda, salt and baking powder. Add strawberries and mix well. Pour mixture into 2 greased and floured 4x8 loaf pans. Bake for one hour at 350 degrees.

SIMPLE STRAWBERRY JAM

1 pound strawberries, stems removed and cut into ½-inch pieces
½ cup sugar

Place strawberries and sugar in a medium saucepan over medium heat. Stir constantly until bubbling and thickened, approximately 10 to 15 minutes. Pour into a glass jar and cool completely. Store in the refrigerator for up to 1 week. Makes 1½ cups.

CANNING

There are two primary methods of canning: a hot water bath and a pressure cooker. Glass jars made especially for canning are reusable and come in various sizes.

For neutral or acidic foods, such as fruits, pickles, jams, jellies, fruit butter and sauerkraut, the hot water bath canning method is sufficient. For this method, no special equipment is needed, other than a big pot and the canning jars and lids. It is handy to have either a jar rack or a jar lifter for grabbing jars out of the hot water.

For any foods that are low acid, such as meats, seafood, milk and all fresh vegetables (with the exception of tomatoes), the pressure canning method is best. This is because these foods are not acidic enough to prohibit the growth of bacteria, which could cause food poisoning. The pressure and heat generated by the cooker are usually effective in killing any harmful bacteria.

Always wipe down the rims of the jars after filling and before the lids and rings are applied. This ensures a tight seal.

Strawberry Pie

Adapted from a recipe submitted by Emily of Se-Em-Da Farms.

3 cups strawberries, cut into bite-size chunks
1 cup cold water
1 cup evaporated cane juice or sugar
2 tablespoons organic cornstarch
Pat-in-Pan Pie Crust or crust for 1-crust pie

Mash ½ cup of the strawberries with a potato masher. Set the rest of the strawberries aside. Combine the mashed strawberries and water in a medium saucepan and bring to a boil. In a separate bowl, combine the evaporated cane juice or sugar with the cornstarch. Add the dry sugar mixture to the saucepan and bring to a boil, stirring constantly. Turn down the heat and simmer until liquid becomes thick. Remove from heat and fold in the strawberries. Carefully pour the filling into the crust. Chill and serve cold.

Strawberries can easily keep frozen. Rinse strawberries and remove stems. Lay them out in a single layer on a cookie sheet and place the cookie sheet in the freezer until individual strawberries are frozen. Finally, take the strawberries off the cookie sheet and place in freezer storage containers.

Strawberry Rhubarb Pie

This recipe was submitted by Whittaker Berry Farm in Ida, Michigan.

1½ cups sugar
3 tablespoons quick-cook tapioca
¼ teaspoon salt
¼ teaspoon nutmeg
1 pound or 3 cups cut rhubarb (½-inch-long pieces)
1 cup sliced strawberries

1 tablespoon butter
Pie crust

In a large bowl, combine sugar, tapioca, salt and nutmeg. Add rhubarb and berries. Mix well to coat the fruit. Let stand for 20 minutes. Spoon mixture into pie shell and dot with butter. Top with a lattice crust. Bake at 400 degrees for 35 to 40 minutes.

> Squash is often labeled as summer or winter squash. Summer squash—like zucchini, crookneck squash and yellow squash—has a thin skin and should be eaten shortly after picking. Winter squash—such as Hubbard squash, butternut squash and acorn squash—has a thick skin and can be stored in a cool basement for several months.

Baked Squash Seeds

Saving the seeds from large squash and baking them with salt and seasoning makes a tasty snack.

Start by pulling the seeds from the meat of the squash. Lay the seeds out on a large towel and use another towel to wipe away the coating. If a little meat still clings to the seeds, do not worry, as it will bake up along with the seeds. Place the seeds in a bowl and generously coat them with olive oil. Sprinkle salt over the coated seeds. If desired, add some favorite spices, like curry powder, cayenne, cumin or ginger. Mix well and place coated seeds on a baking sheet. Roast at 350 degrees for approximately 12 to 15 minutes, or until toasted and brown. Turn seeds several times during baking to help them bake evenly.

Baked Acorn Squash

Acorn squash is a winter squash that is acorn shaped. Most acorn squash is dark green with a deeply ridged outer skin. Inside, the squash has a deep yellow to orange flesh that is about six inches long.

1 acorn squash
2 tablespoons butter
2 teaspoons honey or pure maple syrup
2 tablespoons Sucanat

Preheat oven to 375 degrees. Cut squash in half lengthwise (from stem to end). Using a spoon, scoop out the seeds from the center of each squash half. Score the insides of each half several times with a knife. Add 1 tablespoon of butter, 1 teaspoon of honey or maple syrup and 1 tablespoon of Sucanat to each hollowed-out squash half. Place each half in a large baking dish, cut side up. Add approximately ¼ inch of water to the bottom. This helps keep the squash moist. Bake for approximately 1 hour, or until the flesh is tender. Remove from oven and let cool. Spoon any butter-sugar sauce that has not been absorbed by the squash over the exposed areas. Makes 2 servings.

Ground cinnamon, raisins and other dried fruits, chopped nuts, salt, pepper or herbs can be added for different variations of baked acorn squash.

Sweet Potato Casserole

This recipe for Sweet Potato Casserole was submitted by Betty Jeffers. It is a family favorite that she makes every year.

3 cups mashed sweet potatoes
¾ cup sugar
½ cup milk
½ cup butter, melted
2 eggs, well beaten
1 teaspoon vanilla extract

Topping
1 cup brown sugar
½ cup flour
½ cup milk
¼ cup butter, melted
1 cup chopped pecans

Combine mashed sweet potatoes, sugar, milk, butter, eggs and vanilla and pour into a 2- to 3-quart buttered casserole dish. Combine topping ingredients and pour over mixture. Bake for 30 to 40 minutes in a 350-degree oven.

SWEET POTATO CHIPS

Sweet potatoes
Salt

Peel sweet potatoes and cut into thin slices. Spread on mesh screen of a food dehydrator, sprinkle with salt and dehydrate until crispy, according to food dehydrator instructions.

SWEET POTATO PIE

2 large, red-skinned sweet potatoes, cooked and mashed (should yield about 1½ cups)
1 cup Sucanat
1 cup whipping cream
3 eggs
1 teaspoon vanilla extract
¾ teaspoon ground cinnamon
¼ teaspoon ground nutmeg
¼ teaspoon salt
1 9-inch pie crust

Mix together all ingredients and transfer filling to crust. Bake pie until filling is set in center, about 45 minutes. Cool, cover and refrigerate.

TACO SEASONING MIX

1 tablespoon chili powder
1 teaspoon salt
½ teaspoon onion powder
½ teaspoon paprika
½ teaspoon cumin

Mix spices in ½ cup of water. Add to a pound of browned and drained ground beef and let simmer.

Tomatoes are versatile—they can be stuffed, baked, boiled, stewed, pureed, deviled, glazed, pickled, grilled or fried. Consider canning or freezing tomatoes for later use. They can be used in soup, chili and spaghetti sauce.

Tomatoes with Hickory Smoked Sea Salt

This recipe was submitted by Tammy Saunders from T & J Cottage Gourmet.

1 dozen Roma tomatoes, cut into quarters
½ cup olive oil
1 tablespoon hickory smoked sea salt
1 tablespoon cracked black pepper

Preheat oven to 300 degrees. Cut tomatoes and place on a baking sheet with raised sides. Drizzle olive oil over the tomatoes and sprinkle the tomatoes with the hickory smoked sea salt and cracked black pepper. Bake for 45 minutes.

Freezing the Harvest

If freezer space is ample, stocking up on seasonal fruits and vegetables is easy to do. Some produce, such as most berries, cherries, rhubarb and tomatoes, can be frozen with little fuss. Other produce, such as carrots, corn, green beans, peas, broccoli, bell peppers and asparagus, requires blanching before freezing. Blanching is quickly cooking the produce in boiling water for a couple of minutes. The short dip in hot water kills bacteria and halts the action of food-degrading enzymes.

After washing, cutting and preparing the produce for the freezer, the produce should be placed out on a large baking sheet and allowed to harden in the freezer. Each piece can be popped off the baking sheet and placed in freezer bags or freezer storage containers. This method keeps all the pieces from freezing together. This way, whatever serving size is needed can be taken out of the container or bag easily.

Tomato Relish

Tomato relish can be served with grilled meat, poultry or fish.

2 medium tomatoes, finely chopped
½ medium onion, minced
½ cup cider vinegar
2 teaspoons sugar
Salt to taste
Ground pepper to taste
2 tablespoons chopped fresh basil leaves (or 2 teaspoons dried crushed basil leaves)

Combine all ingredients in a medium bowl. Use all at once or store in a sealed container in the refrigerator for up to 1 week. Makes approximately 4 servings.

To Peel Tomatoes

Bring a pan full of water to a boil. Cut an X in the bottom of each tomato. Use a slotted spoon and place a tomato in the boiling water for 30 seconds. Remove tomato with the slotted spoon and place in ice water. With a sharp knife, the loosened skin will peel off easily.

Trail Mix

Create a custom trail mix by using any combination of the following:

Almonds
Cashews
Unsweetened shredded coconut
Dried fruit
Peanuts
Pecans
Pretzels
Raisins
Semi-sweet chocolate chips
Sunflower seeds
Walnuts

Vegetable Lasagna

Recipe submitted by Liberty Local Market.

3 cups vegetables
½ pound lasagna noodles (approximately nine noodles)
1 egg
15 ounces ricotta cheese
½ cup Parmesan cheese
Chopped parsley, to taste
8 ounces Meadow Maid mozzarella cheese, shredded
4 cups spaghetti sauce

Preheat oven to 350 degrees. Dice and steam 3 cups of vegetables. Set steamed vegetables aside to cool. Boil 9 lasagna noodles according to package directions, drain and cool slightly. In a medium bowl, beat the egg and mix in the ricotta cheese, ¼ cup Parmesan cheese and parsley.

To assemble the lasagna, spread 1 cup of sauce on the bottom of a 9x13 baking dish, cover with 3 noodles, spread the noodles with half the cheese mixture, layer half the vegetables, 1 cup mozzarella and 1 cup sauce. Add 3 more noodles and repeat the layers from the first layer. Top with 3 more noodles, spread with remaining sauce, Parmesan and mozzarella. Cover the dish with foil and bake for 1 hour. Remove the foil and bake for an additional 10 minutes. Let cool for 10 minutes before serving.

> When making casseroles, lasagna, etc., double the recipe and freeze the extra. The extra will be ready to defrost and cook on busy days.

SALT AND VINEGAR CHIPS

Potatoes
Organic apple cider vinegar
Sea salt

Peel and slice potatoes. Place in a large bowl with enough apple cider vinegar to cover them. Soak for 15 minutes. Drain and lay potato chips on the mesh screen of a dehydrator. Dehydrate until crispy, according to food dehydrator manual.

VINAIGRETTE SALAD DRESSING

This is a classic salad dressing recipe submitted by Liberty Local Market.

¼ teaspoon paprika
¼ teaspoon dry mustard
⅛ teaspoon ground pepper
1¼ teaspoons salt
2 tablespoons lemon and herb or balsamic vinegar
2 tablespoons lemon juice
2 tablespoons water (optional)
¾ cup olive oil
1 peeled garlic clove (optional)

Put dry ingredients in a bottle or jar with a tight-fitting lid. Add vinegar, lemon juice and water. Mix well. Add oil and garlic. Shake well before serving. Makes a little more than 1 cup of salad dressing.

Zucchini can be frozen and used later in recipes. To store grated zucchini in the freezer, wash each zucchini thoroughly and peel if desired. Cut the top and bottom ends off and shred the zucchini in a food processor or food grater. Fill freezer containers with pre-measured amounts and label the container. The pre-measured amounts can be easily defrosted when needed for recipes such as zucchini bread and zucchini cookies. Once thawed, the pre-measured amount can be added to the recipe just as fresh zucchini would be. The liquid in the container is natural juice from the zucchini and can be used in the recipe.

Yeasted Sugar Cake

This cake is a great alternative for shortcake or served with fruits.

¼ cup warm water
2¼ teaspoon active dry yeast
¼ evaporated cane juice
2 cups all-purpose flour
½ teaspoon salt
½ cup warm milk
2 eggs, room temperature
4 tablespoons butter, softened

Topping
2 tablespoons butter, softened
¼ cup evaporated cane juice

Stir together ¼ cup warm water, yeast and 1 teaspoon of evaporated cane juice in a small bowl. Let stand for about 10 minutes, until foamy. In a mixing bowl, combine flour, remaining cane juice and salt. Add the yeast mixture, milk and eggs and beat until smooth. Add butter and mix until batter is silky. Scrape down the sides of the bowl, cover and let batter rise until doubled, about 45 minutes. Lightly butter a 9-inch cake pan. Pull out dough and shape into a flat disc. Set disc in pan and flatten to the edge of the pan. Rub soft butter over the top and sprinkle evaporated cane juice over the buttered surface. Cover and let rise for 30 minutes. Preheat the oven to 400 degrees during the last 10 minutes of rise time. Bake for 20 to 25 minutes. Serve warm. Yields approximately 10 servings.

Zucchini Beef Skillet

This recipe was submitted by Ilene Fruth of Fruth's Sugarhouse Greenhouse & Floral.

1 pound ground beef
1 large onion, chopped
1 cup green pepper, chopped
1 clove garlic, minced
1½ teaspoon salt
¼ teaspoon ground pepper
1 teaspoon chili powder
3 cups zucchini or summer squash, sliced
2 large tomatoes, peeled and chopped
¼ cup fresh whole kernel corn (about 3 medium-sized ears)
2 tablespoons pimientos, chopped
¼ cup fresh parsley

Sauté beef, onion, green pepper and garlic in a 12-inch skillet until well browned. Add remaining ingredients. Cover and simmer for 10 to 15 minutes, or until vegetables are tender. Makes 6 servings.

> Brown several pounds of ground beef at once. Freeze one-pound sections for later use in tacos, chili, etc.

Zucchini Spinach Soup

3 tablespoons olive oil
1½ cups onion, chopped
1 tablespoon chopped garlic
¼ teaspoon salt
1 cup sweet bell pepper (any color), seeded and chopped
2½ cups zucchini, chopped

4 cups vegetable stock
4 cups fresh spinach leaves
1 cup fresh sweet basil, chopped

Heat olive oil in a large pot over medium-high heat. Sauté onions, garlic and salt until vegetables start to soften. Stir in pepper, zucchini and vegetable stock. Bring to a simmer and cook approximately 10 minutes, or until pepper is soft. Add spinach and basil and stir until soft. If desired, use an immersion blender to blend until smooth. Serve hot. Makes about 6 servings.

Zucchini Bread

3 eggs, beaten
2 cups Sucanat
1 cup olive oil
1 tablespoon vanilla extract
3 cups all-purpose flour
3 teaspoons cinnamon
2 teaspoons salt
½ teaspoon baking powder
2 cups zucchini, grated

In a large bowl, beat eggs, Sucanat, olive oil and vanilla until thick. In a separate bowl, combine flour, cinnamon, salt and baking powder and mix thoroughly. Add dry mixture and zucchini to the sugar mixture and mix well. Pour into greased loaf pans and bake at 325 degrees for 1 hour, or until a knife inserted in the center comes out clean.

Zucchini Chips

Zucchini
Soy sauce
Garlic or onion powder

Thinly slice zucchini. Dip in soy sauce and lay on the mesh screen of a food dehydrator. Sprinkle with garlic or onion powder and dehydrate until crispy, according to the food dehydrator manual.

Zucchini Chocolate Chip Cookies

1 egg, beaten
½ cup butter, softened
½ cup Sucanat
⅓ cup honey
1 tablespoon vanilla extract
1 cup zucchini, finely shredded
1 cup unbleached flour
1 cup whole wheat flour
½ teaspoon baking soda
¼ teaspoon salt
¼ teaspoon cinnamon
1 cup chocolate chips

Combine egg, butter, Sucanat, honey, vanilla and zucchini in a large bowl. Set aside. Combine flours, baking soda, salt and cinnamon in a separate bowl. Combine wet and dry ingredients. Stir in chocolate chips and mix well. Drop by spoonful onto a greased baking sheet and flatten with the back of a spoon. Bake at 350 degrees for approximately 12 to 15 minutes. Makes about 2 dozen small cookies.

Zucchini and Feta Salad

One medium zucchini, cut into matchsticks
Sea salt
Extra virgin olive oil
Black pepper, freshly cracked
Crumbled feta cheese

Place zucchini in a colander in the sink. Sprinkle lightly with salt and toss to coat. Allow zucchini to sit for about 20 minutes to draw out extra moisture. Place zucchini in a mixing bowl, drizzle with olive oil, top with a bit of cracked black pepper and top with feta cheese. Serves 2.

What Is in Season in Ohio?

Harvest times vary each year due to temperatures and weather. Also, those with greenhouses and hoop houses are able to extend growing seasons for a variety of fruits and vegetables.[62]

apples: August through October
arugula: May through September
asparagus: mid-April through June
basil: July through September
beans (fava): May
beans (horticultural): early July through September
beans (lima): early July through September
beans (pole): late June through September
beans (snap): early June through September
beets: June through mid-October
blackberries: mid-July through August
blueberries: July into August
broccoli: June and mid-September through October
Brussels sprouts: August through November
cabbage: June through October*
cantaloupe: August and September
carrots: July through October*
cauliflower: mid-August through October
celery: mid-July through October
chard: May through September

cherries: late-June through July
cilantro: June through September
collards: mid-May through mid-October
corn (sweet): July through September
cucumbers: July through September
currants: July
eggplant: mid-July through September
endive and escarole: June through mid-October
garlic: August through November
gooseberries: mid-June through mid-July
grapes: August and September
green beans: July through September
green onions: June through September
herbs (various): May through October
kale: June through mid-October
leeks: August through October
lettuce (various): mid-May through October
melon: July through September
mustard greens: mid-May through mid-October
okra: mid-July through mid-September
onions: August through October*
parsley: early June through October
parsnips: September and October*
peaches: mid-July through early September
pears: August through mid-October
peas: mid-June through July
peppers (bell): July through mid-October
peppers (hot): late July through mid-October
peppers (sweet): mid-July through early-October
persimmon: October
plums: September
potatoes: July through early-November*
pumpkins: mid-September through October
radishes: mid-May through October
raspberries (black): mid-June into July
raspberries (fall): mid-August and September
raspberries (red): mid-June into July
rhubarb: mid-April through June
scallions: June through September

shelling beans: September through October*
spinach: mid-May through mid-July and mid-August to mid-October
squash (summer): mid-June through September
squash (winter): mid-August through November*
strawberries: June
tomatoes: July through early October
turnip greens: mid-May through mid-October
turnips: August through early-November*
watermelon: August through September
zucchini: July through mid-October

*Root crops, cabbage and potatoes may be stored through the winter in a root cellar. Some root vegetables, like carrots and beets, can be left in the ground until it is time to harvest. Shelling beans are available dried year-round.

What Is a CSA?

A CSA, or Community Support Agriculture, provides consumers with another way to buy local, seasonal food directly from the farmers. Through the growing season, some farmers offer CSA shares, which typically consist of produce the farmer grows. By purchasing a share of a CSA, consumers receive a box of seasonal produce each week or every other week.

A CSA provides the consumer with a direct relationship to the farmer growing his or her food and the opportunity to learn how to cook in season with fresh produce. At times, the box may contain unfamiliar items, providing an opportunity to learn how to prepare them or use them in a dish. If the box is overflowing with items that cannot be consumed right away, the produce can be frozen, pickled, canned or made into jam—all ways to preserve the food for later.

Currently, two vendors at the Toledo Farmers' Market provide CSA packages. Sage Organics and Jentzen Farms offer reasonably priced shares that can be picked up on Saturday at the market.

Visiting the Toledo Farmers' Market

Visiting the Toledo Farmers' Market for the first time or just returning for a visit? Here are some things to consider:

*The Toledo Farmers' Market is located at 525 Market Street. Upon arrival, begin looking for a parking place on adjacent streets, as the market lot is often full.

*The Toledo Farmers' Market has an on-site office and handicapped accessible restrooms on the side closest to the Libbey Glass Outlet.

*Especially in warm weather, keep a cooler in the car to keep items cold on the way home.

*Take cash, preferably small bills and change. Most vendors have change for large bills, but smaller bills make it easier for everyone. The Toledo Farmers' Market can accept major credit cards and Ohio Direction Cards. Participating vendors accept coupons from the Senior Farmers' Market Nutrition program and WIC coupons.

*Even though most vendors have bags, a reusable shopping bag that fits comfortably over the shoulder is always helpful. Open baskets with a comfortable handle can be useful for carrying fragile items, such as berries, cookies and eggs.

*Some shoppers like to make a loop around the market before buying anything and take mental notes of who is selling what. However, if there are only a few items left, the vendors might be sold out after a stroll around the market.

*Do not hesitate to ask about the products being sold. If they have time, the farmers may be able to suggest ways to prepare unfamiliar produce.

*Many organic farmers choose to forgo the certification process because they have small farms and the certification is expensive. Nevertheless, many farmers grow their crops sustainably, following organic farming standards. Remember, farmers often feed their own families the food they raise, so they may be inclined to reduce their usage of chemical and synthetic fertilizers and pesticides.

*Farmers' market produce is more fragile than produce found at big box stores. The produce at the market is picked when it is at its peak of freshness, while most of the produce at the local grocery is picked underripe so it can ripen during transport or storage. Refrain from squeezing the fruits and vegetables at the market. They can be easily bruised. Also, avoid over handling produce due to sanitary reasons. When smelling for freshness, hold the produce near the nose, not against it.

*Do not dig fingernails into the kernels of an ear of corn. This is unsanitary, and if not purchased, the ear will have to be thrown out due to health reasons. If the end of the ear of corn feels full, it is fully ripe, and there is no need to pull down the husks to check for plump kernels.

*It is great to run across friends at the market, but try to not block the aisles or the vendors' stalls while you chat.

*Buy large quantities if you find something you like. Take a little extra time and freeze or preserve your favorite produce and enjoy it year-round.

*Look over the events schedule on the Toledo Farmers' Market website at ToledoFarmersMarket.com. Throughout the year, there are special events, entertainment, auctions, Slow Food demonstrations, taste-off competitions, cook-offs and canning demonstrations.

*The Toledo Farmers' Market is behind the Libbey Glass Outlet and Superior Antique Mall. Plan a few extra minutes if you have any additional shopping.

*Take a break from the market and enjoy the Riverwalk along Swan Creek.

Painting by Melinda Hallenbeck.

Epilogue

As soils are depleted, human health, vitality and intelligence go with them.
—Louis Bromfield

Writing this book was an amazing journey for me. I met several families who have been in farming and growing for decades and have seen plenty of change through the years. I came into the project with many questions about the future of our food system, but unfortunately I have very few answers. I can see where so many aspects of our food system are skewed.

In visiting the local markets, it is hard for me to understand that local food sales—including CSAs, farmers' markets and direct sales—make up fewer than 2 percent of all food sales. It is difficult to believe that only 2 percent of the food eaten in Ohio is grown in Ohio when a drive through the countryside reveals field after field of crops growing. However, most fields are corn and soybean destined to be hauled away and converted into animal feed or processed into a multitude of ingredients like high fructose corn syrup, vegetable oil or a variety of other additives. In fact, only 1 percent of the corn grown in this country is grown to be eaten as corn.[63]

The agricultural practices used in most large fields today are stripping the soil of nutrients and producing food with less nutritional value than that grown years ago. Researchers claim that produce "found in today's supermarket is anywhere from 5% to 40% lower in minerals (including magnesium, iron, calcium and zinc) than those harvested just 50 years ago."[64] Excessive pesticide use results in insects resistant to the chemicals used. Even pesticides banned in America are still made, exported and used in other countries that produce fruits and vegetables sold back to the United States in grocery stores.[65] Pesticides have been linked to attention deficit hyperactivity disorder, or ADHD, a condition affecting nearly 4.5 million children in the United States, half of whom are taking medication for the condition.[66]

Since the introduction of genetically modified foods in the mid-1990s, there has been "a 265 percent increase in the number of hospitalizations related to food allergies."[67] The latest research now claims that one in twelve American children now has food-related allergies. These allergies are thought to be the result of genetically altered ingredients in food, which make up about 75 percent of products on grocery store shelves. Approximately 91 percent of soy and 85 percent of corn grown in the United States is genetically modified, and what is not processed into food is fed to animals destined to be consumed by humans.[68]

Growing up in the Southwest, I drove past feedlots frequently. I felt sorry for those who lived in proximity to those disgusting and smelly places. However, I never made the connection between those feedlots and filthy cows and my food. Now I see such a striking difference between those crowded pens of cows standing in their own excrement and the pastured cows my farming friends tend. The cattle in feedlots are there to be fattened up as cheaply as possible.

Of course, at each level, there will be people who will argue over practices and standards. People like to think that the United States Department of Agriculture and the Food and Drug Administration are safeguards of our food production system; however, they do not have a foolproof system. *Consumer Reports* sampled chickens from different stores and found that over half of the pathogens found in the chickens were resistant to one or more antibiotics.[69] It is believed that this sort of resistance is a result of animals consuming feed containing antibiotics and rendered animals that have been treated with antibiotics. Therefore, the animals build up a resistance to several antibiotics. This is not uncommon. Most animals in big industry are eating feed made from rendered animals. This is a way to provide cheap protein and to recycle parts from butchered animals that are not normally processed and sold at grocery store meat counters. Antibiotics are also added to feed as a preventative measure because animals are in crowded conditions ripe for the spread of disease.

Some people, like me, find many of these practices at factory farms appalling. However, there are people who turn a blind eye because they feel like there is nothing they can do about it. Others do not care. Once, when talking about cheap chicken prices, my husband, who has his own favorite pet chicken, was faced with a disturbing response. "I wish they would cram more chickens into a pen so it would be even cheaper," a woman exclaimed. She, like the industry, has come to no longer view animals as animals but rather as production units. People seem to forget that animals undergo stress and can get sick under such unnatural conditions. That is why many animals are fed antibiotics in their feed. This is not just the case with chickens; it happens in all industrial meat processing.

It is no wonder that we, as a nation, are ill. Americans face rising rates of obesity, type 2 diabetes, heart disease and other food-related maladies. Approximately 66 percent of Americans are clinically overweight. By 2008, the Centers for Disease Control and Prevention, or CDC, estimated that one-half of Americans used at least one or more prescription drugs, while one in ten used five or more. One out of every five children used one or more prescription drugs. Many of these drugs included prescriptions for ADHD, depression, high cholesterol and high-blood pressure.[70]

The CDC estimates that five thousand Americans die each year because of foodborne pathogens. When food is processed in large factories and contamination occurs, it can be deadly, affecting thousands who have come in contact with the food. Contamination can occur at any level—from the animal, often raised in unfit conditions, to the processing, packaging and storage. This is what happens when we leave large corporations in charge of our food. Rather than support our local farmers and eat wholesome real foods, Americans consume 62 percent of their calories from processed foods—foods more than likely containing genetically altered ingredients, foods grown without regard to the negative impact they may have on the environment, foods that have devastating effects on health and foods controlled from start to finish by large corporations.[71] Here in Northwest Ohio and Southeast Michigan, we are lucky to have the resources to grow and produce what we need. There are farmers who raise produce and animals in the traditional way. They practice sustainable agriculture, raising healthy animals and nutritious foods. They have held fast against the changes when their farming neighbors were either getting bigger, buying large equipment and growing monoculture crops, or giving up and seeking other jobs.

I have visited farms and greenhouses in this area that produce plenty of plants. One of the large local growers I visited transports plants to non-chain businesses in area states. I pressed for more information and discovered that large mega chain stores—like Walmart, Home Depot, Lowe's, etc.—rarely buy from local producers. They order from large wholesalers who have several "growing stations" throughout the country. There are a lot of resources wasted to transport crops from other states when Ohio and Michigan can supply our needs. Honestly, it does not make sense to me.

Even the large grocery store chains, which essentially squeezed the life out of small grocers, are now threatened by the large mega stores. In 2006, CBS News reported that fifteen cents of every grocery dollar was being spent at Walmart.[72] Studies go on to say that 20 percent of American women shop at Walmart at least once a week.[73]

There are plenty of arguments about productivity and food security. There are more arguments about how we are expected to feed a growing population. However, lack of food does not appear to be from lack of production but rather from unequal distribution of food. Defenders of genetically engineered crops claim that technology can feed the hungry. But if this were the case, companies developing the seeds would be

Eleanor Billau saved articles and took many photographs of the market through the years. Her collection became invaluable to the making of this book, and many of her photos, like this one, have been used to help illustrate the history of the market. Eleanor once wrote, "We will never outgrow our need for fresh fruits, vegetables, plants, flowers, baked goods, fresh eggs, and poultry that is available at the market."

more concerned about creating crops that would provide nutrition for people—seeds that do not require expensive equipment and chemicals and seeds without restrictive licensing—rather than crops intended as feed for animals or processed foods. It seems our attention would be better spent trying to reduce wasted food and find innovative ways to distribute it. Jonathon Bloom, who studies food waste, points out that Americans waste more than 40 percent of the food produced for consumption.[74] Waste happens in restaurants, grocery stores and homes. Waste even happens in the fields, when food is left unpicked due to nonuniformity or the fact that it would not survive harvesting, boxing and transport. Food waste ultimately drains resources that go into producing crops: water, time and fossil fuels used for irrigation, spraying and transportation. In the case of processed food, more resources are consumed with additional transportation and packaging.

There are some who will say that the problem is too big and there is nothing we can do, that what little can be done is like a drop of water in the ocean. However, that will not stop me from doing what is best for my family's health and for the earth to the best of my abilities. I wish to support sustainability and create healthy meals for my family. I want to support the true stewards of the land and waste little. I want to know my farmers and know what their animals eat and how they tend their fields and farms. I will continue to shop at the market, and I hope I will see you there.

Notes

Acknowledgements

1. There are some strong opinions regarding the use, or lack thereof, of an apostrophe in farmers' market. If the market is for farmers, then it would be written farmers market. However, if it is a market owned by farmers, it would be possessive and be written farmers' market. Unfortunately, such phrases are ambiguous, and a writer is left guessing whether it is appositive or possessive. Also, style guides do not agree. While AP style does not use an apostrophe after the *s*, the Chicago Manual of Style does. The debate continues. The Toledo Farmers' Market is run by an association made up of vendors, thus lending itself to the plural possessive use of an apostrophe. So, for consistency in this book, the possessive is used throughout.

Introduction

2. Mark Hyman, "How Eating at Home Can Save Your Life," *Huffington Post,* January 9, 2011.
3. Dean Foods controls about 40 percent of the national milk supply. David Goodman, "The Future of Milk," *Eating Well* (July/August 2010). The company does business under several brand names, which include Price's, Meadow Gold, Reiter, Country Fresh, Horizon Organic and more. Dean Foods brands found at www.deanfoods.com/brands.aspx (accessed June 16, 2011).

FARMERS' MARKETS

4. Mary Alice Powell, "Farmers' Market Is More than a Place to Buy Produce," *Toledo Blade*, June 6, 1999.

THE WAY OF THE FARMER

5. "History of the Shopping Cart," Real Cart, www.realcart.com/history (accessed July 4, 2011).
6. Doris Eggleston, *Growing Up With Featherbeds, Kerosene Lamps, and Potbelly Stoves* (N.p.: Xlibris Corp, 2001).
7. Barbara Krasner-Khait, "The Impact of Refrigeration," *History Magazine*, www.history-magazine.com/refrig.html (accessed June 30, 2011).
8. *Time*, "The New American Farmer," November 6, 1978, www.time.com/time/magazine/article/0,9171,948286-1,00.html.
9. "Concentration in the Food Industry," Corpwatch, community.corpwatch.org/adm/pages/food_industry.php (accessed July 17, 2011).
10. Dan Fesperman and Kate Shatzkin, "The Plucking of the American Farmer," *Baltimore Sun*, February 28, 1999.
11. Karen Charman, "Genetically Engineered Foods: Promises & Perils," *Mother Earth News* (October/November 2002), www.motherearthnews.com/Real-Food/2002-10-01/Genetically-Engineered-Food-Promises-and-Perils.aspx.
12. "*Bacillus thuringiensis*," University of California, San Diego, www.bt.ucsd.edu/synthetic_pesticide.html (accessed July 13, 2011).

TOLEDO FARMERS' MARKET HISTORY

13. The year 1832 is debatable. Nothing has been uncovered to prove the date, but at the same time, no one can disprove it. An early photograph of the market on Superior Street is thought to be from 1888. Some of the earliest mentions of the market were found in farming and business publications in 1912 and 1913. Ralph E. Phelps, "Market: Monroe St. Area a Food Center for 124 Years," *Toledo Blade*, June 9, 1956.
14. Phelps, "Market."
15. Sterling Beeson, "Toledo's Municipal Market," *Municipal Journal*, August 8, 1912.

16. Paul A. Leidy, "New Market in Toledo," *Worchester Magazine* 15 (1912). Paul A. Leidy also mentioned that "Toledo has had a municipal market for a good many years." He wrote that it was self-supporting, having "netted a revenue of some few thousand dollars each year."
17. Arthur Hastings Grant and Harold Sinley Buttenheim, *The American City*, vol. 8 (Toledo, OH, 1913).
18. Joseph J. Flanagan, "Public Given Profit in Manager Plan of Operation," *Toledo Times*, August 29, 1937.
19. *Toledo Blade*, "Hucksters Buy at New Market: Clean Out Producers Early Before Women Get Chance to Purchase," July 12, 1913.
20. It was difficult to determine how long the Superior Street market continued. On market applications from as early as 1939, there were only three markets listed, and the Superior Street market was not among them.
21. Swan Creek was navigable during this time and was utilized as part of the canal that went to the Maumee River. Old maps reveal that there was a meandering loop, or oxbow, in the portion of the creek where the current Toldeo Farmers' Market is today. It may be that by the time it was filled in, that portion of the creek was no longer used and the creek had changed its course. A Toledo map in 1918 showed the loop of the oxbow, while one from 1919 showed the loop gone and Superior Street extended.
22. Flanagan, "Public Given Profit."
23. Woman Alive! Coalition, "Market Began on Spielbusch in 1939," *Bend of the River*, clipped article found in Eleanor Billau's collection, date unknown.
24. Larry Wagner, "When I Went Home with My Great-Grandfather We Ate Lunch and Just Talked!" *Archbold, Ohio: Farmland News*, May 4, 2004.
25. Mark Zaborney, "Ex-Eatery Bore Woman's Name," *Toledo Blade*, clipped article found in Eleanor Billau's collection, date presumed to be after March 13, 1988.
26. Wagner, "When I Went Home."
27. *People's Voice, People's Savings Association*, "See You at Clara's!" 1978 (third quarter).
28. Elsie Cram, "Rows of Empty Stalls Lend Bleak Air to City's Once-Busy Farmers' Market," *Toledo Blade*, June 25, 1961.
29. *Toledo Blade*, "Farmer's Market Arouses Ghosts of Former Days," July 20, 1969.
30. *Toledo Times*, "Retail Produce Market Entering Season Of Plenty," August 17, 1962, 13.

31. *Toledo Blade*, "Farm Group, City Ratify Market-Rental Pact: Double Income, Self-Support Expected, Under Terms Favoring Larger Producers," February 17, 1971.
32. *Toledo Blade*, "Gross Halts Moves to Close Farmers Market after Protests," November 26, 1970, sec. D, 1.
33. "'Silent Spring' Ahead for Farm Market Blighted by City's Fund, Space Crises," clipped article found in Eleanor Billau's collection, possibly from the *Toledo Times* before November 23, 1970, judging by other clippings.
34. "Council Unit Wants Shift in Farm Market Delayed," December 8, 1970, clipped article from an unknown paper found in Eleanor Billau's collection.
35. *Toledo Blade*, "Farm Group, City Ratify Market-Rental Pact," February 17, 1971.
36. *Toledo Blade*, "Fair Market Deal?" February 19, 1971.
37. "5,000 Produce Seekers Jam Farmer's Market," clipped article from an unknown paper found in Eleanor Billau's collection. The year 1973 is written in ink on the article, and I'm estimating the article to be from early August.
38. Bob Nash, "Farmers' Market Relic, Yet Stays Forever Fresh," *Toledo Blade*, August 12, 1979.
39. Ibid.
40. Mary Alice Powell, "The Fresh Scent of Dill Says 'Farmer's Market,'" *Toledo Blade*, August 13,1980.
41. More than likely, the stalls were sinking into the soil because this area was part of Swan Creek and was filled in years before. There were different figures concerning the number of stalls in use at the time. Many vendors rented several stalls, while other stalls were in disrepair.
42. "Stall Replacement, Advertising Among Farmers Market Plans," clipped article from an unknown paper found in Eleanor Billau's collection. The date of publication is also unknown but is assumed to be 1986.
43. *Toledo Blade*, "Farmers Market Begins 48th Year in Operation," April 1, 1986.
44. Jeff Harrington, "Vendors Urged to Fund Promotion," *Toledo Blade*, May 2, 1986.
45. Ned Bell, "Farmers Market Faces Unripe Future," *Toledo Blade*, July 8, 1986.
46. Ned Bell, "Market-Head-to-Be Inherits Work Fast," *Toledo Blade*, June 10, 1987.
47. *Toledo Blade*, "City Drafting Plans for Improvements at Farmers Market," January 15, 1988.

48. *Toledo Blade*, "Upgrading Backed For Farmers Market," September 2, 1988.
49. Dave Murray, "Council Votes More Money to Rebuild Farmers Market," *Toledo Blade*, March 20, 1991. Although the market was not completely built to the initial plans that were drawn, the placement of stalls ultimately made it difficult for some vendors to pull in and out of their assigned stalls with their vehicles.
50. *Toledo Blade*, "Farmers Market Project Resembles Barn Raising," January 3, 1990.
51. *Toledo Blade*, "U.S. Studies Outdoor Farmers Market," May 23, 1991.
52. Ohio Department of Agriculture, "Cottage Food Production Operation," www.agri.ohio.gov/foodsafety/docs/CottageFoodOperation-factsheet.pdf (accessed July 3, 2011).
53. Ibid.
54. Mention of creating a corporation to lease and operate the market was apparent as early as the Toledo Farmers' Market Association annual fall meeting in 1986.
55. *Toledo Blade*, "Farmers Market Tilling New Areas for Growth," May 3, 1994.
56. *Toledo Blade*, "This Little Lizard Went…Market's Opening Offers Array of Attractions," May 22, 1994.
57. "Area Seniors & Farmers to Get $1.2 Million Federal Boost with Introduction of 'Farmers Market Coupons,'" press release from congresswoman Marcy Kaptur, January 29, 2001. The counties were specified in a letter written on February 23, 2001, and sent to the individual vendors of the Toledo Farmers' Market.
58. *Toledo Blade*, "Voucher Program for Produce a Hit with Area Seniors, Farmers," November 25, 2003.

VENDORS

59. Peter Ross, "Hungarian Zucchini Custom Raised in Toledo," *In the Neighborhood: Cleveland Heights, Shaker Heights, University Heights*, July 14, 1994.
60. Jody Shee, "A Glimpse of Cleveland: Strategies to Differentiate," *The Packer*, www.thepacker.com/fruit-vegetable-news/fresh-produce-retail/a_glimpse_of_cleveland_strategies_to_differentiat_122007804.html (accessed July 4, 2011).

Recipes

61. "Eggs Lower in Cholesterol than Thought: Study," *CBS News*, February 8, 2011, www.cbsnews.com/stories/2011/02/08/earlyshow/health/main7329038.shtml

What Is in Season in Ohio?

62. The list of seasonal produce was put together from charts provided by *Ohio Proud* and *Our Ohio*.

Epilogue

63. Corn Farmers Coalition Fact Book, www.cornfarmerscoalition.org/factbook (accessed June 16, 2011).
64. M.J. Stephey, "Eating Your Veggies: Not as Good for You?" *Time*, February 18, 2009, www.time.com/time/health/article/0,8599,1880145,00.html.
65. John Robbins, *The Food Revolution: How Your Diet Can Help Save Your Life and Our World* (San Francisco: Conari Press, 2011), 332.
66. Sarah Klein, "Study: ADHD Linked to Pesticide Exposure," CNN Health, www.cnn.com/2010/HEALTH/05/17/pesticides.adhd/index.html (accessed July 8, 2011). Studies reveal that produce grown locally and sold at farmers' markets contain fewer trace amounts of pesticides, even when not organic.
67. Robyn O'Brien, *The Unhealthy Truth* (New York: Broadway Books, 2009), 16, 87. There are twelve plants approved for commercial production in the United States that have been genetically altered: corn, cotton, potatoes, tomatoes, soybeans, canola, sugar beets, rice, flax, squash/zucchini, papaya and chicory (radicchio).
68. Jennifer Grayson, "Eco Etiquette: Is Genetically Modified Food Linked to Kids' Food Allergies?" *Huffington Post*, June 22, 2011, www.huffingtonpost.com/jennifer-grayson/eco-etiquette-is-genetica_b_882238.html (accessed July 11, 2011).
69. *Consumer Reports*, "How Safe Is that Chicken? Most Tested Broilers Were Contaminated," January 2010, www.consumerreports.org/cro/magazine-archive/2010/january/food/chicken-safety/overview/chicken-safety-ov.htm.

70. Centers for Disease Control and Prevention. "Prescription Drug Use Continues to Increase: U.S. Prescription Drug Data for 2007–2008," www.cdc.gov/nchs/data/databriefs/db42.htm (accessed June 21, 2011).
71. John Robbins, "How Bad Is McDonald's Food?" *Huffington Post*, October 8, 2010, www.huffingtonpost.com/john-robbins/how-bad-is-mcdonalds-food_b_754814.html (accessed July 11, 2011).
72. Cynthia Bowers, "History of Grocery Stores," CBS News, June 14, 2006. CBS News also pointed out that ten thousand grocery stores have shut their doors in the last two decades.
73. Haley Sweetland Edwards, "4 Million Bananas: Walmart by the Numbers," June 23, 2011, www.mentalfloss.com/blogs/archives/91893 (accessed June 29, 2011).
74. Wasted Food, www.wastedfood.com (accessed June 29, 2011).

Selected Bibliography

Bell, Ned. "Each Farmers Market Is a Little Different." *Toledo Blade*, September 7, 1986.

———. "Farmers Market Enjoys 'Debut' in Downtown." *Toledo Blade*, August 22, 1986.

———. "Plan to Privatize Farmers Market to Go to Council." *Toledo Blade*, March 10, 1993.

Berry, Wendell. *Bringing It to the Table: On Farming and Food*. Berkeley, CA: Counterpoint, 2009.

Blake, Erica. "Flower Day Weekend to Bloom." *Toledo Blade*, May 25, 2006.

Bowers, Cynthia. "The History of Grocery Stores." CBS News, June 14, 2006. www.cbsnews.com/video/watch/?id=1060362n.

Bunch, Ryan, and Jason Webber. "Market Stock: Plowing Toledo's Farmers' Market." *Toledo City Paper*, June 28–July 5, 2005.

Conkin, Paul K. *A Revolution Down on the Farm: The Transformation of American Agriculture Since 1929*. N.p.: University Press of Kentucky, 2008.

Cram, Elsie. "Rows of Empty Stalls Lend Bleak Air to City's Once-Busy Farmers' Market: Cold, Rainy Spring, Health Regulations Blamed by Vendors." *Toledo Blade*, June 25, 1961.

Davis, Karen. *Prisoned Chickens, Poisoned Eggs: An Inside Look at the Modern Poultry Industry*. Summertown, TN: Book Publishing Company, 2009.

Deemer, Danielle. "April Profile: Ralph Schlatter." Ohio Ecological Food & Farm Association. www.oeffa.org/profiles-april2010.php.

Eggleston, Doris. *Growing Up with Featherbeds, Kerosene Lamps, and Potbelly Stoves*. N.p.: Xlibris Corp, 2001.

Grant, Arthur Hastings, and Harold Sinley Buttenheim. *The American City*. Vol. 8. Toledo, OH, 1913.

Hoff, John. "Dixie Food Sold at Toledo Market." *Toledo Blade*. Reprint, "Former Yazooans Sell Southern Food in Ohio," *Yazoo City Herald*, December 31, 1970.

Hyman, Mark. "How Eating at Home Can Save Your Life." http://drhyman.com/how-eating-at-home-can-save-your-life-3576.

Leidy, Paul A. "New Market in Toledo." *Worchester Magazine* 15 (1912).

Murray, Dave. "Life's Not Simply a Walk in the Park for Bill Scalzo." *Toledo Blade*, April 14, 1988.

Nash, Bob. "Farmer's Market Relic, Yet Stays Forever Fresh: The People Make It Special, Sellers, Buyers Concur." *Toledo Blade*, August 12, 1979.

Northwest Ohio Greenhouse Industry Cluster Project. "Collaborating to Compete: The Case of Northwest Ohio's Greenhouse Industry." www.ohiogreenhouse.com/publications/CH05.pdf.

Phelps, Ralph E. "Monroe St. Area: A Food Center for 124 Years." *Toledo Blade*, June 9, 1956.

Planting for Public Spaces. "2007 Individual Market grantees." www.pps.org/markets/2007_individual_market_grantees.

Pollan, Michael. *The Omnivore's Dilemma: A Natural History Of Four Meals*. New York: Penguin, 2007.

Powell, Mary Alice. "Toledo Hucksters Hit the Road with Harvest." *Toledo Blade*, August 23, 1981.

———. "To Market, To Market: Area Farmers Showcase Autumn's Bounty of Fresh Fruits and Vegetables." *Toledo Blade*, October 20, 1998.

———. "To Market, To Market: Fresh Air, Flowers, and Dewy Produce Lure Shoppers to the Outdoor Stalls." *Toledo Blade*, July 5, 1994.

———. "Summertime a Fresh Produce Bonanza in Ohio." *Toledo Blade*, July 17, 1985.

Reiter, Mark. "Gourmet Baker Tastes Success at Sylvania Site: Natural Ingredients Promoted." *Toledo Blade*, July 2, 2007.

Remsey, Duane. "Local Couple Makes and Markets Bullfrog BBQ Sauce." *Toledo Free Press*, February 27, 2011.

Rodale, Maria. *Organic Manifesto: How Organic Farming Can Heal Our Planet, Feed the World, and Keep Us Safe*. N.p.: Rodale Book, 2010.

Salatin, Joel. *The Sheer Ecstasy of Being a Lunatic Farmer*. Swoope, VA: Polyface Inc., 2010.

Schmid, Ron. *The Untold Story of Milk*. N.p.: New Trends Publishing, 2003.

Seitz, Ali. "Fresh Sweet Corn Provides Market a Recipe for Success." *Toledo Blade*, July 15, 2007.

Smith, Kathie. "Farmers' Markets: Vendors Sell Locally Grown, Homemade Products." *Toledo Blade*, July 25, 2006.

Toledo Farmers' Market. *Farmers' Market Cookbook and Other Good Things: Truly a Piece of Toledo*. Toledo, OH, 1998–1999.

Toledo Times. "Selling Radishes Before the Dawn." June 30, 1935.

Troy, Tom. "Toledo Farmers Market 'Moving' Indoors: Facility's Roll-down Doors Create Year-Round Event." *Toledo Blade*, November 5, 2007.

Tucker, Darryl Q. "Black Farmers Profit by Living Off Downtown Marketplace." *Toledo Journal*, September 18–24, 1991.

United States Department of Agriculture. "Farmers Markets and Local Food Marketing." www.ams.usda.gov/AMSv1.0/FarmersMarkets.

University of Toledo Urban Affairs Center. "Sustainability Family Style: Documenting the Lives of Growers, Gardeners, and Family Farmers in Northwest Ohio." Report compiled from interviews conducted in July 2009.

Vallongo, Sally. "Market Melange: People, Sights, and Sounds are Part of the Refreshing Mix of Open-Air Marketplace." *Toledo Blade*, September 20, 1992.

Worthen, Molly. "Farmers' Market Chief Quits: She Cites Verbal Abuse by Vendors as 1 Reason for Action." *Toledo Blade*, August 1, 2002.

About the Author

Trini L. Wenninger resides in Sylvania, Ohio, with her husband, Ken, and daughter, Leia, and her backyard hens: Topsy, Dorothy, Chippy and Mama Bess. Trini is a member of the Sylvania Area Historical Society and prefers to shop at the local farmers' markets. Having a degree in history and an appreciation for wholesome local food made compiling this book on the Toledo Farmers' Market a perfect fit. Trini's other books include *Images of America: Sylvania*, co-authored with Gaye E. Gindy; *Rose Wilder Lane's San Francisco*; and *Flora of their Writing: The Plants of Laura Ingalls Wilder and Rose Wilder Lane.*